THE TOMB OF THOUTMÔSIS IV

PLATE 1.

WOVEN TAPESTRY BEARING THE PRENOMEN OF AMENÔTHES II.
No. 46526.

MR. THEODORE M. DAVIS'
EXCAVATIONS: BIBÂN EL MOLÛK.

———

THE

TOMB OF THOUTMÔSIS IV,

BY

HOWARD CARTER AND PERCY E. NEWBERRY;

WITH AN ESSAY

ON THE KING'S LIFE AND 'MONUMENTS,

BY

GASTON MASPERO,

Director-General of the Service des Antiquités,
Hon. D.C.L., and Fellow of Queen's College, Oxford; Member of the Institute, and Professor at the College of France;

AND A PAPER ON

THE PHYSICAL CHARACTERS OF THE MUMMY OF THOUTMÔSIS IV,

BY

G. ELLIOT SMITH,

Fellow of St. John's College, Cambridge; Professor of Anatomy, Egyptian Government School of Medicine, Cairo.

———

Duckworth

First published in 1904
by Archibald Constable & Co. Ltd.
Reprinted in 2002 by
Gerald Duckworth & Co. Ltd.
61 Frith Street, London W1D 3JL
Tel: 020 7434 4242
Fax: 020 7434 4420
Email: inquiries@duckworth-publishers.co.uk
www.ducknet.co.uk

Foreword © 2002 by Nicholas Reeves

A catalogue record for this book is available
from the British Library

ISBN 0 7156 3120 9

Printed in Great Britain by Bath Press Ltd, Bath

FOREWORD

'Mr. Theo. M. Davis of Newport, U.S.A., as everyone knows, took a great interest in Egyptian archaeology as well as in Egypt. He came out every year and spent his winters on the Nile in his dahabeyeh "The Bedouin". He often told me that he would like to have some active interest during his sojourns in Upper Egypt. Thus, with Maspero's consent, I put the following proposition to him. The Egyptian Government would be willing, when my duties permitted, for me to carry out researches in the Valley of the tombs of the Kings on his behalf, if he would be willing on his part to cover the costs thereof, that the Egyptian Government in return for his generosity would be pleased, whenever it was possible, to give him any duplicate antiquities resulting from these researches. At the same time I told him of my conjecture regarding the possibility of discovering the tomb of Tuthmosis IV. The Government offer he accepted ...'

(Howard Carter's unpublished 'Autobiographical Sketches', Griffith
Institute, Ashmolean Museum, Oxford, notebook 16, sketch VI,
quoted in Nicholas Reeves and John H. Taylor,
Howard Carter Before Tutankhamun,
London, 1992, p. 71)

The tomb of Tuthmosis (Thoutmôsis) IV was the first pharaonic tomb to be uncovered in Egypt's legendary Valley of the Kings by Howard Carter, Egyptology's most famous excavator. It was a burial whose existence Carter had early rationalized, and whose location he would doggedly stalk. The success of the archaeologist's quest, on 18 January 1904, was to stimulate two fruitful decades of research and excavation – first by the man for whom Carter had found the tomb, Theodore M. Davis, followed by the celebrated partnership of Carter himself and Lord Carnarvon, whose efforts culminated in the discovery of Tutankhamun some eighteen years later.

The discovery of Tuthmosis IV's tomb would not disappoint. Scrambling down the newly revealed, rubble strewn entrance steps for the first time, Carter found himself in a well-cut, sloping corridor. This led down to a deep vertical shaft and, beyond that, a four-pillared room, before turning abruptly to the right to give access to a naively decorated antechamber and the royal burial apartments proper. Here, chaos reigned: the space was strewn with antiquities – *shabti*-figures and model vessels of brilliant blue faience, ritual equipment, textiles, wooden throne panels, and a unique, superbly decorated chariot-body – with the whole dominated by a fabulous sarcophagus of painted quartzite. The king's mummy, of course, was long gone, but Carter knew it well. Carried off by the necropolis guardians for reburial elsewhere around 1000 BC, it had turned up in a side-chamber of the tomb of Amenophis II (KV 35) in 1898 – from which storeroom Carter had arranged it for transfer to Cairo a short time later.

Davis, when he eventually viewed 'his' discovery, was overjoyed. Though the shattered contents of Tuthmosis IV's tomb offered a mere glimpse of the glories Fate still had in store for Carter, the find was an extraordinary one and of enormous archaeological significance. Undisturbed since the closing days of the New Kingdom, it would shed significant new light not only on 18th Dynasty art, architecture and burial customs, but upon the history of the Valley itself — in particular, the phenomenon of tomb-robbery and the State's response (more on which may be found in my *Valley of the Kings: the decline of a royal necropolis* [London, 1990]).

Davis's publication of the find, *The Tomb of Thoutmôsis IV,* first appeared in 1904 in an *edition de luxe* penned by Howard Carter and his friend and mentor Percy E. Newberry, in turn Professor of Egyptology at the Universities of Liverpool and Cairo. It was issued in two versions — the rare full and unexpurgated edition reprinted here, with contributions from Gaston Maspero, Director of the *Service des Antiquités,* and Grafton Elliot Smith, Professor of Anatomy in the Cairo School of Medicine; and an abridged version, lacking the scene-setting introductory matter, which appeared the same year as a volume of the Cairo Museum's *Catalogue général.* The fuller version was, for its day, a splendid work, achieving a standard which Davis's subsequent publications in this important series, sadly, would never match.

London, January 2002   Nicholas Reeves

CONTENTS.

PREFACE.

With keen appreciation of the obligation I am under to the authors of this book, I desire to thank M. Maspero for his learned and comprehensive life of Thoutmôsis IV: Mr. Percy E. Newberry for his valuable contribution to this publication: Dr. G. Elliot Smith for his important Paper on the Physical Characters of the Mummy of Thoutmôsis IV: and especially Mr. Howard Carter for his admirable exploration work, his photographs, and the beautiful drawings of the chariot.

THEO. M. DAVIS.

Newport,
  Rhode Island.

MAP OF THE BIBÂN EL MOLÛK.

LIST OF TOMBS IN THE BIBÂN EL MOLÛK.

1. Ramses X.
2.   „   IV.
3.   „   III.^A.
4.   „   XII.
5. Uninscribed.
6. Ramses IX (?).
7.   „   II.
8. Menephtah.
9. Ramses VI.
10. Amenmeses. (Lunch House.)
11. Ramses III.^B.
12. Mummy pit (uninscribed).
13. Vizier Bay.
14. Tewosret.
15. Seti II.
16. Ramses I.

17. Seti I.
18. Ramses XI.   (Engine Room.)
19. Montouhikhopshouf.
20. Hatshopsouît.
21. Mummy pit (uninscribed).
22. Amenôthes III.   (Western Valley.)
23. Aŷ. (Western Valley.)
24. Uninscribed. (Western Valley.)
25. Uninscribed. (Western Valley.)
26. Mummy pit (uninscribed).
27.   „   „
28.   „   „
29.   „   „

30. Mummy pit (uninscribed).
31.   „
32. Uninscribed.
33.   „
34. Thoutmôsis III.
35. Amenôthes II.
36. Mahiprî.
37. Uninscribed.
38. Thoutmôsis I.
39. Uninscribed.
40. Mummy pit.
41.   „
42. Prince Sennefer.
43. Thoutmôsis IV.
44. Tent-karou.
45. Userhat.

INTRODUCTION.

In January, 1902, Mr. Theodore M. Davis undertook a systematic exploration in the Valley of the Tombs of the Kings for the benefit of the Service des Antiquités. This location being within the jurisdiction of the Inspector-

Fig. 1. Procession of workmen removing the Antiquities
after the opening of the Tomb.

General of the Services des Antiquités, I undertook the direction of the explorations. After consulting with M. Maspero, the Director-General, and Mr. Davis, it was decided to carry out excavations in such a manner as to thoroughly exhaust the small valley running west from Tomb No. 3 (see Map, p. VI), continuing the work right up to the sheer cliff. These excavations were commenced in January, 1902, and resulted in minor discoveries, already chronicled in the Service's "Annales." In the first part of the excavations there was found in the débris, some way up the valley, a small fragment of an alabaster vase, bearing the cartouche of Thoutmôsis IV, which led me to believe I was in the near neighbourhood of the tomb of that king. In January, 1903, the work had reached the base of the cliff, where there were distinct signs of artificial working, and eventually the opening of a tomb was found (see Map, p. VI, No. 43). Here, in the débris, many fragments of antiquities turned up, and, among others, the end of a wooden axe-handle, bearing the name of Thoutmôsis IV. This at once led me to believe that the tomb discovered belonged to this Monarch, and, in clearing down to the surface of the rock, I came upon two small holes which contained complete, undisturbed, sets of foundation deposits bearing the name of the king.

On the 18th January, 1903, the door of the tomb was sufficiently cleared to permit entrance. Unfortunately Mr. Davis had sailed for Assuan, and being unable to reach him by telegraph, I concluded to enter the tomb and make an examination of its contents. I invited Mr. Robb. de P. Tytus to accompany me in my inspection.

After removing the remaining rubbish that covered the entrance, we found that it had been closed with roughly-cut stones, through which we made a small hole to enable us to pass. We then entered, accompanied by the head Reis, finding a passage partially filled with rubbish and strewn with broken antiquities. This immediately indicated to us that the tomb had been anciently plundered. Sliding down the passage over the rubbish for about 30 metres, we found ourselves over a gaping well obstructing further progress. Here we were obliged to wait until our eyes became accustomed to the dim light of our candles before we could see the further side or bottom. Gradually there loomed before us the opposite wall, in which we saw an opening had been cut, and, on finding that the well was very deep, we sent for ladders and ropes. Looking around us we saw that the upper part of the walls of this well were painted with scenes in which the cartouche of Thoutmôsis IV figured prominently. Here was, at last, final evidence of the true ownership of the tomb. Ropes and ladders having been procured, we with difficulty descended on the one side of the well and ascended on the other (the well having but little rubbish in it), and succeeded then in entering through the hole into a rectangular hall with two columns. Fastened round the nearest column to this opening was an ancient cable rope made of palm fibre, knotted at intervals, and with its end hanging down and reaching to the bottom of the well. Here was further evidence of plunderers. This chamber was practically clean and contained but few antiquities, save some unimportant pieces and an inscribed paddle of a boat. In the left-hand corner of this chamber we found a staircase leading into a sloping passage about 20 metres in length, which gave access to a small square chamber. This passage was partially filled with rubbish, which made our descent difficult, stones rolling down at every step.

The chamber we found to be painted with similar scenes to those of the well, with the addition of two hieratic inscriptions on the right-hand wall. Here, again, was a large mass of débris. In the far corner of the left-hand side we found a doorway, partially blocked up with stones, which had been covered with plaster and sealed. Here there were evidences of double

Fig. 2. Lid of Sarcophagus as found.

sealing, there being two distinct seal impressions : one, the original, showing a jackal over nine prisoners, the other evidently later, because on a different plaster and giving the cartouche of the king Horemheb.

Entering through this doorway we found ourselves in a long-shaped pillared hall, the floor of which was covered with rubbish and strewn with antiquities. At the inner end, between the two last columns, we found a short flight of steps leading to the sarcophagus, which was fully inscribed with texts and the king's name. Its lid, which lay beside it, was supported by slabs of stone under three corners, while under the fourth was a beautifully-modelled wooden cow's head (see fig. 2).

On looking into the sarcophagus we found it to be empty, save for two wooden figures, cast in by the ancient plunderers. Turning round and ascending the steps between the two last left-hand columns, the body of a magnificent chariot loomed before us, and beside it the gauntlet of the king (see Plan, p. xxviii, *ch.*). On either side of this hall were two chambers, which we entered and examined in turn.

The first of these (see Plan, p. xxviii, D and fig. 3) we found to contain a mass of broken blue-glazed faïence vases and figures of exquisite colour, and in the right-hand corner, resting in an erect position against the wall, was a

Fig. 3. Interior of Side Chamber D.

denuded mummy of a boy, whose stomach and cage had been ripped open by the ancient plunderers with a very sharp knife (see fig. 3).

The second chamber (see Plan, p. xxviii C) proved to contain fragments of broken jars, with their sealings, and great quantities of grain reduced to chaff.

In the third chamber (see Plan, p. xxviii B) there was a great mass of mummified joints and geese specially prepared for the use of the king's *ka* (see fig. 4).

The fourth chamber (see Plan, p. xxviii A) was empty, save for a mass of mummy linen-bindings, which had probably belonged to the small mummy found in the first chamber, and this was, perhaps, the place where the plunderers had unrolled it.

All these chambers had originally been shut up and sealed, but in no case was a door or stone left in place. The whole tomb was itself in an unfinished state, the objects therein being scattered about all over the floors, and there were remains on stones of oil wicks left by the ancient violators. We then returned to the entrance, and reclosed the tomb, leaving necessary guards to protect it.

After reporting all these facts concerning the discovery and state of the tomb, on the 3rd February, 1903, Mr. Theodore M. Davis, accompanied by M. Maspero and friends, officially opened it, and made a thorough inspection. It then became my duty to make an inventory of its contents and to ensure its safety : in this work Mr. Percy E. Newberry lent me his valuable assistance.

FIG. 4. INTERIOR OF SIDE CHAMBER B.

It is interesting to note that, amongst the antiquities found in the rubbish outside the tomb, there was a small wooden cartouche bearing the name of Thoutmôsis I, and a scarab seal of Queen Hâtshopsîtû. In the foundation deposits occurred an alabaster saucer, bearing the name of the Queen Hâtshopsîtû, usurped by Thoutmôsis IV, and inside the tomb were fragments of usurped alabaster vases of Thoutmôsis III and Amenôthes II. Besides these, there was also a fine piece of a garment of Amenôthes II in woven tapestry, richly ornamented.

HOWARD CARTER,
Inspector-General of the Service des Antiquités,
Upper Egypt.

AUGUST, 1903.

ON

THE LIFE AND MONUMENTS OF THOUTMÔSIS IV,

BY

G. MASPERO.

I.—PARENTAGE.

THOUTMÔSIS IV, who entitles himself on his monuments ⟨hieroglyphs⟩ "The Horus, Mighty Bull, whose diadems are firmly established,"

FIG. 5. THOUTMÔSIS IV AND QUEEN TIÂA.

⟨hieroglyphs⟩, "Lord of the two Goddesses of the South and of the North, Stable in his Kingdoms as Toumou," ⟨hieroglyphs⟩, "The Golden Horus, Powerful of Sword, Destroyer of the barbarians," ⟨hieroglyphs⟩,

"The King Manakhpérourîa," 𓅨⚬⟮𓏤𓏠𓏠𓏠𓈖𓐮𓂧𓂧⟯, "Son of the Sun, Thoutmôsis Khâkhâou," was the son of Amenôthes II, whom he succeeded. An inscription in the tomb of a certain Harmhabi at Cheikh Abd-el-Gournah expressly states that this Pharaoh was his father,[1] but for a long time there was complete ignorance as to his mother's name, until it was conjectured that she was called Tiâa. Two statuary groups are, however, now known to us, in which this queen is represented seated by the side of Thoutmôsis IV, the inscriptions on which inform us that she was *the principal royal wife whom he loves* and *the royal mother*.[2] Before this double discovery it had been inferred, from an inscription in the tomb of Zanni, at Cheikh Abd-el-Gournah, in which she is entitled *royal wife* only,[3] that she was the wife of Thoutmôsis IV.[4] But it at once became evident that the presence of the epithet, *royal mother*, on the statues which represent her seated by the living Thoutmôsis IV is inexplicable on the assumption that she was the latter's wife, for the only actual king of whom she could be mother was he by whom she is represented sitting, *i.e.*, Thoutmôsis IV, and this fact has been recognised by the most recent historians of Egypt.[5] If we put side by side the epithets applied to this queen on the various monuments, we see that she is alluded to as *king's daughter*,[6] *principal royal wife*,[7] *principal royal wife, royal mother*,[8] and if we fill in these royal titles from the time in which she lived, we see that she must have been the royal daughter of Thoutmôsis III, the principal royal wife of Amenôthes II, and the *royal mother* of Thoutmôsis IV. Now another queen, Hâtshepsouîtou II Marîtrî, comes before us under exactly similar conditions. We know that she was the wife of Thoutmôsis III and the mother of Amenôthes II, and the monuments entitle her *great royal wife who loved him, royal mother*.[9] The resemblance

[1] Bouriant, *le tombeau d'Harmhabi*, dans les *Mémoires de la Mission française*, t. V, p. 434.

[2] The first of these statues came from Shodou in the Fayûm, and has been described by Brugsch, *der Möris-See*, in the *Zeitschrift*, t. XXXI, p. 29; the second was discovered at Karnak by Legrain in 1903.

[3] Champollion, *Monuments de l'Égypte et de la Nubie*, t. I, p. 481.

[4] Lepsius, *Königsbuch*, Pl. XXVII, No. 371; Bouriant–Brugsch, *Livre des Rois*, Nos. 347–349.

[5] Wiedemann, *Ægyptische Geschichte*, p. 379; Petrie, *History of Egypt*, 1896, pp. 164, 165.

[6] Lepsius, *Königsbuch*, Pl. XXVII, No. 371a; Bouriant–Brugsch, *Livre des Rois*, No. 348.

[7] Champollion, *Monuments*, t. I, p. 481; *cf.* Lepsius, *Königsbuch*, No. 371; Bouriant–Brugsch, *Livre des Rois*, No. 347.

[8] *Zeitschrift*, Vol. XXXI, p. 29, and the Legrain statue.

[9] Lepsius, *Königsbuch*, Pl. XXVII, Nos. 350b, c, 356; Bouriant–Brugsch, *Livre des Rois*, No. 352.

between the two protocols justifies us in concluding that the latest inter-
pretation given to that of Queen Tiâa is the correct one, and that she really
was the mother of Thoutmôsis IV, and not his wife.

We know for certain then that Thoutmôsis IV was of royal blood on his
mother's side as well as by his father. But was he the natural heir to the
throne? A tomb at Chejkh Abd-el-Gournah, that of Hekernehah, represents,
with Thoutmôsis IV, royal sons whose names are effaced, but who none the
less seem to have been brothers of the sovereign.[1] They must have been
younger brothers or of inferior rank, the offspring of slaves or foreign
women. We nowhere encounter any trace of an elder brother, or of a
younger one holding in virtue of his mother, superior rights. Nevertheless,
it is possible that Thoutmôsis IV was not always heir presumptive to the
throne, and that, until he entered the period of adolescence, his chance of
succeeding his father was but a remote one. This, at least, is what I am
inclined to infer from the terms of the inscription which he himself set up
between the paws and against the breast of the Great Sphinx at Gizeh, the
materialised image of the god Harmakhis. This inscription was discovered
in the year 1818, in the course of Captain Caviglia's excavations round the
Sphinx,[2] and the text was published very soon afterwards by Young.[3] Vyse
republished it twenty-two years after, but with the addition of several errors.[4]
Lepsius brought out another transcript of it with different mistakes, and minus
several fragments, which had disappeared since the time of the discovery.[5]
Birch was the first to attempt an explanation of portions of it in Vyse's work
of 1842, and thirty years later Brugsch translated into German the last lines,
those which are of historical interest.[6] The only two complete versions
extant are those of Birch[7] and of Mallet,[8] both in English. The importance
of this document, both historically and with special reference to the dynastic
succession, was recognised for the first time in the second volume of my
Histoire Ancienne.[9]

[1] Lepsius, *Denkmäler*, III, 69a.

[2] An account of these excavations, written by Salt, was published by Colonel Vyse in his
Operations carried on at the Pyramids of Gizeh, 8°, London, 1842, Vol. III, p. 107 *sqq*.

[3] Young, *Hieroglyphica*, London, 1820, pl. 80.

[4] Vyse, *Operations carried on at the Pyramids of Gizeh*, Vol. III, Pl. 6.

[5] Lepsius, *Denkmäler*, III, 68.

[6] Brugsch, *Der Traum Königs Thutmes IV bei dem Sphinx*, in the *Zeitschrift*, 1876, pp. 80–95.
and *Geschichte Ægyptens*, pp. 394–8.

[7] Birch, *Dream of Thothmes IV*, in *Records of the Past*, 1st Series, Vol. XII, pp. 43–9.

[8] Mallet, *The Stele of Thothmes IV*, in *Records of the Past*, 2nd series, Vol. II, pp. 45, 46.

[9] *Mêlée des Peuples*, pp. 292–4.

It runs as follows :—"The year I, the third month of Shaît, the day 9,
"under the king Thoutmôsis IV, who gïves life, stability and power like Râ
"for ever ! The good god, the son of Toumou, the champion of Harmakhis
"the Sphinx,[1] the life of the Lord of All,[2] the all-powerful fabricator of the
"perfect flesh of Khopri,[3] the Being beautiful of face as the sovereign his
"father, He who in his goings out is furnished with his insignia bearing
"the diadems of Horus on his head, King of the North and the South for
"the gods, very gracious to the divine Enneade ; He who purifies Heliopolis,
"who strikes for the castle of Ptah,[4] who presents Maît to Toumou and who
"raises her towards Rîsanbou'f,[5] who establishes the rites of daily sacrifices
"to the gods, who fulfils all that is and is the being whose *first act*, ☐⊚☐,
"set going *for the first time* the whole creation, when springing forth from
"Nou he came at the voice of the demiurge who summoned him ; who
"searches for all that may be of service to the gods of the South and of the
"**North,**[6] who builds their temples of white stone and establishes the bread of
"**their offerings,** the legitimate son of Toumou, Thoutmôsis, whose risings are
"**as the risings** of Râ, flesh of Horus on the throne of this god Manakhpêrourìa,
"giver of life !

"Now at the time when his Majesty was an infant like Horus who was a
"child at Khebît, when his beauties were such as those [of Horus] the
"champion of his father, when his aspect was like that of the god himself,
"when the soldiers shouted for joy for love of him, when all the royal

---

[1] ⊤⊙ *Naznouîti*, he who fights by word and action for his father Harmakhis, as Horus
did for his father Osiris by arms in his wars against Set, by speech before the tribunal of Gabou.

[2] Osiris.

[3] ⊙ *Ouarou-sapou*, is only imperfectly rendered by the term "All-powerful." ☐⊙ *sapou*
signifies the moment in which an act is accomplished and the act of accomplishing it ; the
sapouou of a being, man or god, are the successive moments of his acts. A god or man is called
Ouarou-sapouou, or "Chief, great in acts," when the acts which he performs are decisive not
only for himself but also for those who depend or proceed from him. Here the king, identified
with the creative deity, is *great in acts* because he makes the flesh of the Sun, and thus causing
him to rise, becomes the primary cause of all the phenomena which were produced on the
primeval chaos by the rising of the sun.

[4] Literally, "striking, striking, by the castle of Ptah," that is to say, he who undertakes
constructive works for Memphis.

[5] *Rîsanbouf*, "South of his wall," is the name of a quarter of Memphis and of the god
Ptah who inhabits it.

[6] The first member of this phrase 〰️ ⌣ *iri ntît nibe*, shows the king rendering to the
gods all that had been given them by his predecessors and which actually existed. The second
⊙ *hehoui Khouît*, presents him to us as searching for an occasion for new foundations
which would be his own particular work.

" children and all the princes were under the spell of his valour because of
" his exploits, for he also had run his course round the world[1] and his
" victories are like those of the son of Nouît [; at that time], he was
" beating the country[2] for his diversion on the mountain of Memphis, from
" the South to the North,[3] shooting at a target with darts of iron, chasing
" lions and gazelles on the mountains, driving in his chariot [drawn] by
" horses fleeter than the wind, with one or other of his servants, unknown to
" all the world ; then, when the hour came to grant a siesta to his servants,
" [betaking himself] to the favourite region of Harmakhis[4] by the side of
" Sokaris in the necropolis of Rannoûtit, of the male gods and of the mother-
" goddesses in heaven, of the mother [divine regent] of the gods of the North,
" the lady of the wall of the South, of Sokhît, the lady of Khasît,[5] the great
" talisman, the mysterious place of the first manifestation for the gods of
" Khriahou,[6] the divine path of the gods towards the western horizon of
" Heliopolis, namely the Sphinx of Khopri the Very-great who reposes in that
" place, the great in souls, the mysterious in terrors[7] the moment that shadows
" fall upon him, towards whom come the palaces of Memphis and the whole
" locality on either side of it, their arms raised in adoration to his face and
" with offerings for his double.

" One of these days it happened that the royal son, Thoutmôsis, having
" come to walk towards the south, and being seated in the shadow of this
" great god, a dream of sleep seized him at the moment when the sun was
" shining on the brow [of the Sphinx], and his majesty found that this god
" was speaking to him with his own mouth, as a father speaks with his son,
" saying : ' Behold me, then ; contemplate me, my son Thoutmôsis, for I

---

[1] Literally, " he had re-iterated the circle." The sun circles victoriously round the world ;
the king, who is identified with the god, *re-iterates his course*, that is to say, conquers the world.

[2] Literally, " he made campaign."

[3] Literally, " on his route, South and North."

[4] The phrase is troublesome, but if we compare it with what follows we see that the
preposition ⟨⟩ *r* depends on the idea expressed by the verb *satoutou* ; the king *walked* as far
as, *towards* the place where was the Sphinx. The word *satpou* which precedes the name of the
god has no determinative ; it is, I believe, a derivative from the root *satapou*, " to choose," here,
" the chosen place."

[5] Khasît is the desert, by preference the Libyan desert, east of the Canopic branch of the Nile.

[6] Babylon in Egypt. Of course it is the Sphinx who is designated by the name of talisman,
etc., and it is curious to find, at this epoch, ideas analogous to those expressed by Arab writers
concerning the Sphinx.

[7] *Cf.* the name of Abou'l Hol, *the father of terrors*, which is given to the Sphinx by the
neighbouring Arabs.

"am thy father Harmakhis-Khopri-Râ-Toumou, and I will grant thee to be
"king upon my throne, prince among the living, wearing the red crown and
"the white crown on the throne of Gabou, the chief of the gods possessing
"the earth in its whole length and its whole breadth, the splendour of the
"eye of the lord of all; revenues at thy disposition from the territory of
"Egypt, large tributes from every foreign country, and a long term of years
"during which thou shalt be the elect of Râ,[1] my face being towards thee,
"while thy [face] shall be towards me and thy heart towards me. Now,
"consider my destiny, so that thou mayest protect my perfect members.
"The sand of the desert has invaded me, that upon which I am: I have
"determined to cause thee to execute that which is in my heart[2] for
"thou art my son, my champion; draw near, I am with thee, I am thy
"father.' When the prince heard these words he marvelled, and he knew
"that they were the words of this god. He kept silence in his heart . . . .
"the temples of this region present their offerings to this god."

Thus, at first, Thoutmôsis IV was styled *royal son* merely, and not *eldest
royal son*, as are the princes who were heirs presumptive to the throne, such,
for example, as Amenmasou, son of Thoutmôsis I,[3] or *royal son and heir*,
as Ramses II, son of Seti I,[4] Amenhiounamif, son of Ramses II,[5] Seti II, son
of Menephtah,[6] or *eldest royal son*, as Amenhikhopshouf, son of Ramses II,[7]
and Phrâhiounamif, son of Ramses III.[8] The omission of all epithets seems
to show that he was merely a prince with no immediate hope of succeeding
his father. It is this circumstance which invests his dream with the aspect
of a prophecy; the god promises to make him king if he on his side will
promise to rid the Sphinx of the sand which encumbered him. Before this
revelation the prince remained silent, which was, no doubt, the best course
for him to pursue. The opening of the history of Sinouhît tells us of the
terror which seized upon that prince when an accident had rendered him

---

[1] Literally, "a duration of the elect of Râ, great in years."

[2] Literally, "I have turned about *sanouni* to make that thou shouldst do that which is in
my heart."

[3] Grébaut, *Inscriptions inédite du règne de Thotmès 1er*, in the *Recueil de Travaux*, t. VII,
p. 142; *cf.* Maspero, *Les Momies royales de Deir el Baharî*, in the *Mémoires de la Mission
française*, t. VII, p. 631.

[4] Lepsius, *Königsbuch*, Pl. XXXI, No. 415; Bouriant–Brugsch, *Livre des Rois*, No. 390.

[5] Lepsius, *Königsbuch*, Pl. XXXIV, No. 424; Bouriant–Brugsch, *Livre des Rois*, No. 498.

[6] Lepsius, *Königsbuch*, Pl. XXXVI, No. 476; Bouriant–Brugsch, *Livre des Rois*, No. 499.

[7] Bouriant–Brugsch, *Livre des Rois*, No. 450. He probably received this title after the death
of his eldest brother, during the years in which he was heir presumptive.

[8] Lepsius, *Königsbuch*, Pl. XXXVIII, No. 498; Bouriant–Brugsch, *Livre des Rois*, 522.

master of a state secret ; he fled on overhearing the recital to his brother
Ousirtasen of the circumstances of the death of their father Amenemhait II.[1]
I think we may infer, from the facts mentioned above, first, that Queen Tiâa
was not heiress in her own right, but only a secondary princess, like, for
example, Maoutnofrît, of Thoutmôsis I, the mother of Thoutmôsis II ;[2] secondly,
that her son, prince Thoutmôsis, was not heir to the throne at the time of
his prophetic dream quoted on the stela of the year I ; thirdly, that he was
probably rather far removed from the throne, since a divine intimation was
necessary to enable him to ascend it.

If, as the autopsy made by Drs. Smith and Keatinge seems to indicate,
he was about twenty-five at the time of his death,[3] he must have been
between fifteen and eighteen at the time of his accession.   This, however, is
a question the answer to which awaits further medical discussion.

II.—THE WARS OF THOUTMÔSIS.

The reign of Thoutmôsis IV was peaceful.   Nubia and the Soudan had
been indissolubly united to Egypt by Ahmôsis and by Amenôthes I, Syria
had been reduced to the status of an Egyptian province, and relations had
been entered into with the States beyond the Euphrates by Thoutmôsis III.
Amenôthes II had quelled the few insurrections which had broken out at the
death of his father, and since that time there had been no serious uprising
against the Egyptian domination.   The empire over Asia and Africa was
firmly enough established to render any great efforts on the part of the
sovereign superfluous.   A little cleverness and prudence was all that was
wanted to enable him to maintain the state of things instituted by his
predecessors.

In the south his activity was not great.   Like all the Pharaohs of the
second Theban Empire, he had from time to time to suppress incursions of
desert tribes.   It is to this that allusion is made in general terms in the
inscription on one of the architraves of the temple of Amada, where he is
entitled " the good god, the truly vigorous one who crushes Koush and has

---

[1] Maspero, *Les Contes populaires de l'Égypte Ancienne,* 1st ed., pp. 96, 97.

[2] Maspero, *Les Momies royales de Deir el Baharî,* dans les *Mémoires de la Mission française,*
t. VII, p. 633–634.

[3] See below, p. XLIII.

"abolished its frontiers as though they no longer existed.[1]" An inscription in a Theban tomb fixes the limit of the Southern Empire at Kalaî, and says that the king went as far as there.[2] We have but few precise dates. The first occurs on a stela on the rocks of Konosso, and is of the year VII, the third month of Pirît, the day 8. The sovereign is represented standing in the centre of the picture with the *pskhent*-crown on his head, raising his battle-axe above two kneeling prisoners, whom he holds by the hair. Behind him stands Queen Araît, in the *rôle* of protecting deity, her left hand raised, her right holding the mace, and hanging at her side ; on her head are the cap and two tall feathers of the goddess Maout. The two divinities to whom the king is offering in sacrifice the two prisoners are, the one Doudoun, Lord of Nubia, to whom he owes his sovereignty over the nomads ; the other, Khasou, the Lord of the West, who grants him all foreign countries.[3] Owing to the loss of the greater part of the inscription, we are unfortunately not able to say who were the two chiefs thus executed, nor to what tribes they belonged.

The second date belongs to the following year, and is found on a stela engraven on a rock at Konosso, in the neighbourhood of the first. The inscription is long, and the only copy of it which we possess up to the present is not altogether satisfactory ;[4] the general drift of it, however, is fairly clear. It relates how : "In the year VIII, the third month of Pirît, the day 2. "Behold, while His Majesty was in the city of the south at the town of "Karnak, his two hands purified with running water, and while the king was "making offerings to his father Amon, because the latter had made him king "for ever and established him for ever on the throne of Horus, news was "brought to His Majesty : 'The Negro is invading the regions of Ouaouaît ; "he has proclaimed a revolt against Egypt, and has gathered around him all "the vagabonds of other countries.' The king having gone peacefully to the "temple about the time of morning, and having made a great offering to the "father who had created his graces, this is how His Majesty himself prayed "before the prince of the gods, consulting him upon the opportunity of going "himself, praying that he would reveal his intentions to him and guide him "in the right course, so that he might do what was pleasing to his double, "like as a father in relation to his son to whom he has given himself "as a protecting wall for him.

[1] Lepsius, *Denkmäler*, III, 69 and *f*, l. 5.
[2] Sharpe, *Egyptian Inscriptions*, 1st Series, pl. 93, ll. 5, 6.
[3] Lepsius, *Denkmäler*, III, 69*e*.
[4] J. de Morgan, *de la Frontière de Nubie à Kom-Ombo*, pp. 66, 67.

" After that His Majesty departed to strike the rebels in the land of
" Nubia, valiant in his barque of Asia, like Râ when he enters into his barque
" Saktît . . . . his steeds pulling strongly, the *élite* of his
" archers and of all his forces walking at his sides in two lines of young
" soldiers, his galleys manned by his servants, the king going up the Nile like
" Sahou, who illumines the country with his favours, men rejoicing for love
" of him, women quitting their occupations. Landing at Ani (Esneh),
" behold all the inhabitants guide him, marching before him, all the gods of
" the south with their insignia went to meet him ; the goddess of Nakhabît
" and of Bouto put upon me the ornaments of royalty ; she enveloped me in
" her arms, and she bound together for me all the barbarians. It happened
" that at the time of the feast of . . . . . iâ, I stopped at the town
" Edfou. The good god (*i.e.*, the king) came out, like Mantou in all his
" insignia, armed with weapons redoubtable as those of Set of Ombos,
" and that which he leaves behind him lives without destruction, without
" battues on the mountains ; [he came out], with two servants who relieved
" one another attending him, without disorder ; but his soldiers come to
" him because of his vigorous sword, and his terrors entered all breasts, for
" Râ has spread abroad his fears in all the countries like [that of] Sakhît
" in an year of plague . . . . he watched and slept not, he scoured the
" mountain of the East, prowling along its paths like the jackal of the South
" in search of his prey, and he found the miserable negroes in a hidden
" valley known to no one. Now, as soon as the people had fled to this
" distant mountain . . . . with their slaves, their cattle and all their
" forage . . . . ." One line only is missing, which warrants us in inferring
that the surprise of the Negroes in the mountains of the East marks the end
of the campaign.

Summing up the data supplied by this inscription, we see firstly, that
Thoutmôsis IV went forth from Thebes ; secondly, that he arrived at Esneh,
then at Edfou ; thirdly, that it was on leaving Edfou that he took the field,
across the mountain of the East, that is to say, in the regions which extend
between the Nile and the Red Sea ; fourthly, that the surprise of the Negroes
in an unknown valley is the grand exploit of his campaign, and put an end
to the state of things of which he had been told ; fifthly, that it was in
celebration of this event that he erected the stela of the year VIII in the
island of Konosso. To put it briefly, the expedition consists of a raid
into the desert which begins at Edfou and finishes beside Assouân. What
the scribe has depicted with so much bombast is simply a clean sweep

of the bands of marauders who had been harassing the subject tribes of Ouaouaît and, perhaps, the frontiers of Egypt. The mention of Edfou as the last station in the valley seems to show that the king took the route of Redésiéh; how far into the desert he went it is difficult to say. The indications he gives of the distant and unknown ouady, where the marauders were cut off with their families, their cattle, and all their forage, might apply to such ravines as that of the Ouady Abrak. The king did not go as far as the Red Sea, for had he done so he would have mentioned the fact. He must have reached Assouân either by the road followed by Golénischeff in 1889, or by one of the almost parallel tracks mentioned by Floyer in his work on the Etbaye.[1]

Is it to one of these two military excursions, or is it to a third expedition, posterior or anterior, that reference is made in the inscription mentioned by J. de Morgan as being situated on the rocks a little to the west of those of which we have just been speaking, but of which he only describes the initial scene?[2] It seems more probable that this refers to a third expedition; but nothing short of the publication of the text can settle the question, when anyone can be found ready to go to the almost inaccessible rocks on which it is engraved to make a copy.

The so-called wars of Thoutmôsis IV, then, in the country of the South, resolve themselves into a few raids against marauding tribes between the Nile and the Red Sea, sometimes as far as Southern Egypt, sometimes as far as Nubia. The representation graven on the body of the chariot,[3] therefore, which depicts him charging masses of foes, is a merely conventional scene designed to render visible to the eye the action of the sovereign in the South as a parallel to his action in the North. The list which we find on the right side of the interior of the chariot, and which comprises a selection of southern tribes, is thus worded : 1. [hieroglyphs]; 2. [hieroglyphs] Kalaî; 3. [hieroglyphs] Miêou; 4. [hieroglyphs] Ilima; 5. [hieroglyphs] Courases, or Kolosso; 6. [hieroglyphs] Diouraik, where Kalaî represents the traditional limit of the empire on this side.

It does not seem that Thoutmôsis IV had occasion to imperil his life in the North any more than in the South. The pictures traced on the body of the

---

[1] Floyer, *Étude sur le Nord-Etbai*, p. 3 et seq.

[2] J. de Morgan, *de la Frontière de Nubie à Kom-Ombo*, p. 68. M. de Morgan confuses this inscription with the one which Lepsius has published, and which is of the year VII; a comparison of the scenes shows us that they are two different inscriptions.

[3] See below, Pl. XI of the present volume.

chariot of the crushing and taking prisoners of the Syrians, has no more real significance than has that which represents the war against the Negroes ; it is simply a common motif of Egyptian decoration. The list given on the left side of the interior of the chariot is likewise a general list, having no particular application to any determinable act of war. It comprises 1. [hieroglyphs] Naharaina ; · 2. [hieroglyphs] Sangara ; 3. [hieroglyphs] Tounipa ; 4. [hieroglyphs], the Shasu ; 5. [hieroglyphs] Kadshi-Kadesh ; 6. [hieroglyphs] Tikhisa ; this latter no doubt in memory of the victories of Amenôthes II. It will be noticed that the name of the Khati does not appear : the Khati at that time not playing a sufficiently important part in Syrian politics to cause them to be enumerated in abridged lists of the northern peoples. The relations between Egypt and the neighbouring nations, the Mitanni and the Baby-lonians, seem to have been uninterruptedly pacific. A letter written by Doushratta, King of Mitanni, to Amenôthes IV, recalls the fact that Thoutmôsis IV asked of Artatama, grandfather of Doushratta, one of his daughters in marriage, and that Artatama consented to the marriage at the seventh asking.[1]

The allusions to Syrian campaigns which we meet with here and there in the Theban tombs or on private stelæ refer, therefore, not to great wars like those of Thoutmôsis III and of Amenôthes II, but to partial revolts, or to acts of brigandage in the vast territory which depended directly on Pharaoh in Asia. Thus we find an Amenôthes who was high priest of Anhouri, saying that he followed his lord into the countries of the South and of the North, when he went to Naharîna and to Kalaî, that is to say, to the regions of the Euphrates on the one side and the plains of Sennar on the other.[2] It is probable that the sovereign made at least one expedition into Asia, and that it is to this visit to the Syrian provinces that reference is made in the mention of a first campaign in a region of which the name is almost entirely effaced, but may easily be restored to Naharina. He brought back from there the booty which he shared with his father Amonrâ. The enumeration of the treasures granted to the god fills a long inscription graven on the east side

---

[1] Jensen, *Die Thontafeln von Tell el Amarna*, No. 21, ll. 16–8, pp. 50, 51.

[2] Sharpe, *Egyptian Inscriptions*, 1st Series, pl. 93, ll. 5, 6. It has been said (Budge, *A History of Egypt*, Vol. IV, p. 79) that the scribe Zanni speaks of a campaign of Thoutmôsis IV in Zahi. The passage alluded to applies to the reign of Thoutmôsis III and not to that of Thoutmôsis IV : with regard to Thoutmôsis IV, Zanni merely states that he served him, without mentioning in what country.

of the wall built round the obelisk of Hatshopsouîtou, on the east of the great hypostyle-hall at Karnak.[1]

Summing up the above, we see that, neither in the North nor in the South, did Thoutmôsis IV have to undertake any campaigns comparable to those of his grandfather, or even his father.

III.—THE ADMINISTRATION, THE MONUMENTS AND THE FAMILY OF THOUTMÔSIS IV.

The tombs of the Theban functionaries who lived or died under Thoutmôsis IV are particularly rich in information as to the higher administration of Egypt. That of Zanni, one of the scribes who wrote the *Annals* of Thoutmôsis III, shows us the operations of numbering the people and of recruiting the army under Thoutmôsis IV.[2] The same operations are figured in the tomb of Harmhabi, with scenes depicting the envoys of foreign princes, Asiatic and African, bringing presents from their masters to Pharaoh.[3] Nothing in these representations is peculiar to the time of Thoutmôsis IV; they depict the usages and customs common to the whole of the XVIIIth Dynasty, and there is, therefore, no necessity for dwelling upon them here.

Thoutmôsis IV was not a great builder: he carried on the works of his predecessors apparently without any great activity, and he began no work of any importance; this fact, no doubt, is connected with the shortness of his reign. Thebes, as we should have expected, is the town in which has been preserved the greatest number of his monuments. He completed there certain portions which had been begun by Thoutmôsis I. and Thoutmôsis III,

[1] Mariette, *Karnak*, Pl. 33 and text, pp. 56, 57. Naharina is the most probable restoration for that time. Brugsch (*Geschichte Egyptens*, p. 393) restores Kheta, which is not so likely to be correct at that time, since Kheta does not figure on the list given on the chariot (see p. XXIII); he speaks, nevertheless, of "des ersten Feldzuges des Königs gegen das Land Cheta." Petrie (*A History of Egypt*, Vol. II, p. 168) has adopted the restoration suggested by Brugsch, and inserted it in his text, without perceiving that it makes double play with the probable campaigns to Naharina.

[2] Champollion, *Monuments de l'Égypte et de la Nubie*, Vol. I, pp. 484–7, and 830–2; Scheil, *Le tombeau de Djanni*, in *Mémoires de la Mission française*, Vol. V, pp. 591–603.

[3] Bouriant, *Le tombeau d'Harmhabi*, Pl. IV, in the *Mémoires de la Mission française*, Vol. V, pp. 416–34.

amongst others that near the fourth pylon ; these were afterwards restored, and the cartouches of the king re-cut by the first Ethiopian king of the XXVth Dynasty, Shabakaou.[1] The excavations of the winter 1902—1903 have proved that his labours in this locality were more considerable than had previously been supposed. Not only did he build this gate of the fourth pylon, but he re-touched the walls, paved the ground, and placed statues there. It was there that M. Legrain found in January, 1903, the charming group now in the Cairo Museum, which represents him seated by the side of his mother Tiâa (see Fig. 5, p. xiii). When verifying the paving-stones and turning them up to see that they did not rest on still older constructions, we were surprised to find that the blocks of which they are composed were taken from a building of Amenôthes II. On them are depicted some very curious scenes which are evidently the prototype of the representations of the triumph of Seti I ; the stones found up to the present figured the return of Amenôthes into Egypt, and the sacrifice of the chiefs whom he had taken prisoners before Amon. We are tempted by certain indications to think that the bas-reliefs had been used as materials for a pavement by Thoutmôsis IV, which may mean that the monument to which they belonged was either left unfinished at the death of the sovereign or destroyed by his successor. The hypothesis of a destruction by Thoutmôsis IV is very unlikely, in view of what we learn from other monuments regarding his sentiments towards his father. Moreover, M. Legrain found in the month of February of this year the lower part of the famous stela, in which Amenôthes II recounts his Syrian campaign ; the two last lines, the only ones which are approximately intact, state that Thoutmôsis IV has completed his father's stela. It is most unlikely that he would have shown himself so pious in one direction and be so impious in another.

Besides Thebes, the Saîd and Nubia have still some fragments of buildings bearing the name of Thoutmôsis IV. At El Kab he began the small temple which was completed by his son, Amenôthes III.[2] He also carried on works on the island of Elephantine, whither his military raids seem to have led him several times.[3] The temple of Amada, whose reconstruction had been undertaken by his father, occupied him considerably, and his name may be read there on the architecture as well as in the interior of the

[1] Lepsius, *Denkmäler*, III, 69*d* ; Mariette, *Karnak*, text, p. 28.

[2] Lepsius, *Denkmäler*, III, 80*b*.

[3] J. Morgan, *de la Frontière de Nubie à Kom-Ombo*, p. 115.

halls.[1] In Middle Egypt and the Delta his name rarely appears ; the only work of any importance by him which we know of in these regions is the clearing of the Great Sphinx. He dug away the sand in which it was buried up to the neck, and erected against its breast the stela which we translated above ;[2] that was the least he could do for the god who had made him king.

We know little about his family. The names of two only of his queens—Araît and Moutemouaou—are given on the monuments. The reading, Araît, for the name written 𓂋𓏭𓆗, is, to say the least of it, doubtful : it is the current transcription of the sign of the common uræus, but here we might read the name of one of the uræus-goddesses, Rannouît or Marîtsakro, for example.[3] She was a princess of high rank, for she was *royal daughter, royal sister, great royal wife*, and this is all we know about her. The same cannot be said of another of the wives of Thoutmôsis IV, she who was the mother of Amenôthes III. This queen was not called *royal daughter*, hence it is probable that she was not a member of the royal family. The son born of this union, Amenôthes, was, however, heir to the throne, and it was in order to legitimatize his elevation that, according to the customary usage, a intervention on the part of Amonrâ has been supposed ; the god came down to the queen in the likeness of Thoutmôsis, united himself to her and disappeared, leaving her enceinte of a child of pure solar blood, who re-established the purity of the race. The question has lately been raised whether Moutemouaou was not the wife of Amenôthes II, and consequently, if Amenôthes III was not the brother, rather than the son of Thoutmôsis IV. The answer to this question is given on the monuments. At Luxor, in the scene of the theogamy, it is stated that the god Amon came towards the queen under "the form of the Majesty of this husband Thoutmôsis IV."[4] At El Kab Amenôthes III states that he completed the little temple as "a monument of his father Thoutmôsis IV." The terms are sufficiently explicit to expel all doubts : Thoutmôsis IV was certainly the husband of Moutemouaou and the father of Amenôthes III.

---

[1] Champollion, *Monuments de l'Égypte et de la Nubie*, Pl. XLV, 6, and Vol. I, pp. 96–100 ; Lepsius, *Denkmäler*, III, 69, *f–i*.

[2] See p. XVI–XVIII of the present volume.

[3] Mr. Petrie thinks that the uræus "may be merely an ideograph signifying *the goddess-queen*, and designates Mutemua" (*A History of Egypt*, Vol. II, p. 170). He says "that this is all the more probable, since the supposed Arat was *great royal wife*, like Mutemua" (*id.*, p. 174).

[4] 𓈖𓆣𓅭𓏥 𓅓𓏏 𓂻 𓐍𓇋𓇋𓎡𓈖 𓏏𓊹𓎡 𓈖𓈖 (𓇳𓌳𓁐𓏏) 𓈖𓋹, Gayet, *Le Temple de Louxor*, Pl. LXXI, fig. 205, in the *Mémoires de la Mission française*, Vol. XV.

Of other children that he may have had we know one only, a prince Thoutmôsis, who is mentioned on a scarab on an inscription in the island of Sehel.[1] Was this the prince who, dying a little before or at the same time as his father, was deposited in one of the secondary vaults of the hypogee, and whose mummy, violated already in antiquity, was re-discovered standing against the wall? It seems to be that of a child from six to eight years old, and this uncertainty as to age prevents us from knowing whether this prince was older or younger than Amenôthes III.[2]

The reign of Thoutmôsis IV lasted nine years and eight months only, if we are to believe the tradition handed down by Manetho.[3] The date of the year VIII, which has been preserved for us in the stela of Konosso,[4] is within the limits indicated by the tradition. The figures in the Greek lists, however, are generally speaking so inexact, that we must not repose too great confidence in them. We will merely say, therefore, that his reign was short, and that it lasted about a decade, without more specific mention of the number of years. When it closed the child of Moutemouaou was still very young, and his mother must have exercised the regency, at any rate nominally during his minority. This is in fact what we are given to understand by the titles which Amenôthes III gives to his mother in the temple of Luxor. He calls her : " the sovereign princess, very gracious, sweet of love, mistress of " all the countries, mistress of the South and of the North, the Royal mother " Moutemouaou." [5]

G. MASPERO.

CAIRO,
  June 9th, 1903.

---

[1] Wiedemann, *Ægyptische Geschichte*, p. 378; J. de Morgan, *de la Frontière de Nubie à Kom-Ombo*, p. 90, No. 86.

[2] See p. x of the present volume.

[3] Nine years according to Africanus and Eusebius; nine years and eight months according to Josephus.

[4] See above, p. xx.

[5] [hieroglyphs], Gayet, *Le Temple de Louxor*, Pl. LXIX, fig. 197, 198, and Pl. LXX, fig. 199.

PLAN.

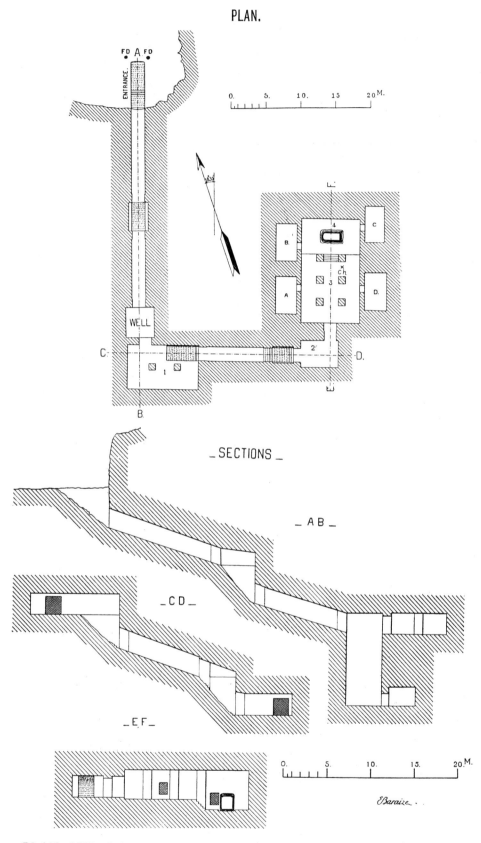

_ SECTIONS _

_ A B _

_ C D _

_ E F _

PLAN AND SECTIONS OF THE TOMB OF THOUTMÔSIS IV.

DESCRIPTION OF THE TOMB AND SARCOPHAGUS OF THOUTMÔSIS IV,

BY

PERCY E. NEWBERRY.

GENERAL DESCRIPTION OF THE TOMB.

THE tomb of Thoutmôsis IV is cut out of the living rock, beneath one of the steep limestone cliffs which line the eastern side of the valley of the Biban el Molûk at Thebes (see Map, p. VI, Tomb No. 43). The descent into it is made by a flight of steps cut in the floor of a small natural platform at the base of the cliff. In this platform, immediately in front of the tomb, are two shallow holes, which contained the foundation deposits buried in sand (see Plan and Sections, p. XXVIII, F, D). The entrance doorway is without any architectural features, and leads directly into a long sloping passage, which gives access to (1) a steep flight of steps with long narrow recesses on either side, and (2) another long sloping passage. At the end of this second sloping passage is a doorway leading directly into a large square well, having a small and low Rectangular Chamber at the bottom of its eastern side. In the inner side of the well, high up in the wall, is cut a doorway, which leads to a Rectangular Hall (marked 1 on the Plan, p. XXVIII), the roof of which is supported by two square pillars arranged longitudinally along its axis. Cut in the floor of the left-hand inner corner of this hall is a steep flight of steps leading down through (1) a sloping passage and (2) another steep flight of steps, with very narrow recesses in the walls on either side, to a doorway giving access to a Rectangular Anti-Chamber (marked 2 on the Plan, p. XXVIII), with low, flat ceiling and well-finished walls. Leading out of this chamber from a doorway cut in its left-hand wall and near its inner end, is a Large Rectangular Sepulchral Hall (marked 3 on the Plan, p. XXVIII), the high ceiling of which is supported by two rows of three square pillars each, arranged longitudinally on either side of its axis. At the inner end of it, immediately behind the third row of pillars, the floor has been sunk to a depth of about one metre, and access is obtained to this lowest part of the tomb (marked 4 on the Plan, p. xxviii) by a flight of five steps cut in the rock between the two last pillars of the hall. In the centre of this sunken part rests the sarcophagus on slabs of stone in a roughly-hewn and very shallow hole. On either side of the hall are small doorways (two on either side) leading to small and low-ceilinged rectangular chambers (marked on the Plan A, B, C, D, p. xxviii).

It is probable that wooden doors were used to close the different compartments of the tomb, but these have all been stolen by the ancient plunderers, and no evidence remains of them except their socket holes and a wooden lintel to the doorway of Chamber A. After the doors had been shut they were roughly sealed round their edges with mud-plaster. In the case of the entrance to the first Rectangular Hall the doorway was completely walled up with stones, which were carefully faced with plaster and coated with a layer of fine stucco. This final layer was then coloured grey, and a painted scene was begun upon it, so as to conceal all traces of the opening to the burial chambers behind, and thus deceive would-be violators of the sarcophagus and robbers of the contents of the tomb. The entrance to the Large Rectangular Sepulchral Hall containing the Royal Sarcophagus was also walled up, and then plastered over, but the plaster, in this case, was stamped all over by a large stamp-seal bearing the design of a jackal over

nine prisoners, arranged in three rows: . It is important to note that before the seal was pressed upon the plaster it was coated with blue paint, the surface of it was then wiped clean, leaving the colour only in the incised parts; it was then applied to the damp material, which consequently received, not merely an impression, but a *coloured* impression,[1] of the seal.

THE PAINTINGS.

Only two of the chambers of the tomb contain paintings: these are (1) the upper part of the Square Well, and (2) the Lower Rectangular Anti-Chamber (Plan, Chamber 2, p. xxviii). In both cases the walls have been

---

[1] We have here the earliest known instance of " block printing."

carefully smoothed and the surface prepared to receive the paintings by being coated with a thin layer of fine grained stucco. After this layer of stucco was put on the artist measured up the walls, prepared his scheme of design, and "flicked" his guiding lines by means of a string saturated with red paint.

Square Well. *Ceiling.* Ornamented with stars painted yellow on a blue ground to represent the sky at night.

Left-hand wall. Frieze, the usual *kheker* ornament, with row of coloured rectangles below. Beneath this frieze is a long and narrow ⊏⊐-sign, extending the whole length of the wall, and coloured blue, with a single row of yellow stars upon it. Below are six scenes, showing gods and goddesses presenting symbols of life (☥) to King Thoutmôsis IV, each scene being accompanied by an explanatory inscription. Beginning on the left-hand side these scenes show :—

    (1) Thoutmôsis IV before Osiris, Khent-Amentıu.
    (2) Thoutmôsis IV before Osiris, Lord of Abydos.
    (3) Thoutmôsis IV before Anubis, the Great God, Lord of the Sacred Land.
    (4) Thoutmôsis IV before Hathor, Lady of the Western Desert.
    (5) Thoutmôsis IV before Hathor, Chieftainess of the Western Desert.
    (6) Thoutmôsis IV before Hathor, Lady of the Western Hill.

Inner wall. The painting covers only the left-hand end of this wall, and consists of the usual *kheker* frieze, an unfinished ⊏⊐-sign, and an unfinished scene with only the figure of Anubis painted in. The remaining walls of this chamber are not painted.

Lower Rectangular Anti-Chamber. *Ceiling.* Ornamented with stars painted yellow on a blue ground to represent the sky at night.

Left-hand wall. Frieze, the usual *kheker* ornament, with row of coloured rectangles below. Beneath this frieze is a long and narrow ⊏⊐-sign, extending the whole length of the wall, and coloured blue, with a single row of yellow stars upon it. Below are four scenes, showing gods and goddesses presenting symbols of life (☥) to King Thoutmôsis IV, and each scene is accompanied by an explanatory inscription. Beginning at the left-hand side these scenes show :—

    (1) Thoutmôsis IV before Osiris, Khent-Amentiu.
    (2) Thoutmôsis IV before Anubis, Within the Temple.

(3) Thoutmôsis IV before Hathor, Lady of the Western Desert.

(4) Thoutmôsis IV before Hathor, Chieftainess of the Western Desert.

Below the scene is a plain dado, bordered above by yellow, red, yellow, and black bands, each band being divided by thick black lines.

Innermost wall (Fig. 6). Frieze, the usual *kheker* ornament with row of coloured rectangles below. Beneath this frieze is a long and narrow ⊏⊐-sign, extending the whole length of the wall, and coloured blue, with a single row of yellow stars upon it. Below are five scenes, showing gods and goddesses presenting symbols of life (☥) to King Thoutmôsis IV, each scene

FIG. 6 WALL PAINTINGS IN ANTI-CHAMBER.

being accompanied by an explanatory inscription. Beginning at the left-hand side these scenes show :—

(1) Thoutmôsis IV before Hathor, Chieftainess of the Western Desert.

(2) Thoutmôsis IV before Anubis, Upon his Hill.

(3) Thoutmôsis IV before Hathor, Chieftainess of Thebes, Lady of Heaven, and Mistress of the Two Lands.

(4) Thoutmôsis IV before Osiris, Khent-Amentiu.

(5) Thoutmôsis IV before Hathor, Chieftainess of Thebes, Lady of Heaven, and Mistress of the Two Lands.

Below the scene is a plain dado, bordered above by yellow, red, and yellow bands divided by thick black lines. The border of coloured rectangles enclosing the two ends of the scene are unfinished.

The remaining walls of this chamber are not painted.

HIERATIC INSCRIPTIONS.

Two hieratic inscriptions have been written in black ink on the unpainted plaster which covers the right-hand wall of the Lower Rectangular Chamber (Plan, Chamber 2, p. xxviii). Both inscriptions are written in bold and

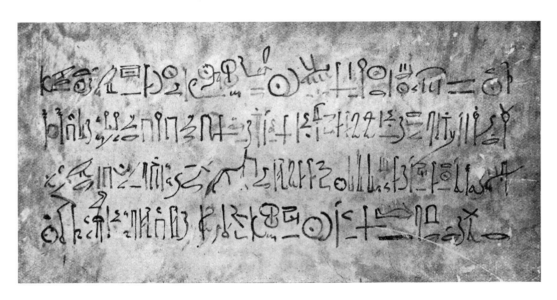

FIG. 7. HIERATIC GRAFFITO No. 1.

large hieratic characters, and relate to an inspection of the tomb that was made by certain Egyptian officers in the eighth year of the reign of King Horemheb. In Figs. 7 and 8 are given photographic reproductions of these two inscriptions, and the following are their transcription and translations :—

No. 1.

(3) [hieroglyphs]

(4) [hieroglyphs]

(1) "The Year VIII, the third month of the summer season under the Majesty of the King of Upper and Lower Egypt, Zeser-kheperu-Ra, Chosen of Ra, Son of Ra, Horemheb, beloved of Amen,

(2) "His Majesty, *L.P.H.*, ordered that it should be recommended to the fanbearer on the left of the King, the Royal Scribe, the Superintendent of the Treasury, the Superintendent of the Works in the Place of Eternity (*i.e.*, the tomb, here the Biban el Molùk),

(3) "The Leader of the Festival of Amen in Karnak, Maŷa, son of the Doctor Auï, born of the Lady Urt,

(4) "to renew the burial of the king Thoutmôsis IV, justified in the Precious Habitation in Western Thebes.

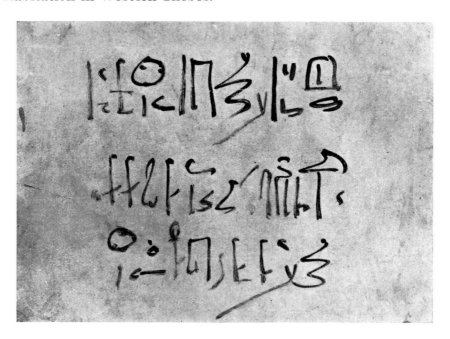

Fig. 8. Hieratic Graffito No. 2.

No. 2.

(1) [hieroglyphs]   (1) "His Assistant, the Steward of Thebes,

(2) [hieroglyphs]   (2) "Thoutmôsis, son of Hat-aaŷ.

(3) [hieroglyphs]   (3) "His Mother Yuh of the City."

THE SARCOPHAGUS.

THE SARCOPHAGUS.

SARCOPHAGUS.—Red Crystalline Sandstone.—Length 3 m.—Width 1·60 m.—
Height 2 m.—Chamber 4.

The Sarcophagus is hewn out of a solid block of stone in the form of a box : its lid being cut out of a separate piece. Both box and lid are rounded at the head and square at the feet. The upper side of the lid is of a curved form. The whole of the outer surface is covered with incised figures and inscriptions, painted in yellow, as follows :—

Lid. Down the centre of the lid is a vertical line of hieroglyphs reading :—

From this vertical line are eight horizontal bands of hieroglyphs (four on either side), written vertically and running from the centre to the edge of the lid and down the sides of the coffin. These lines read :—

On the left-hand side, counting from the head :

(1)

(2)

(3)

(4)

On the right-hand side, counting from the head :

(5)

(6)

(7)

(8)

Box.—On the curved end of the sarcophagus are, one horizontal and eighteen vertical, lines of inscription; with a standing figure of Nephthys with arms upraised and wearing the ⬚-sign upon her head, in the centre, between the ninth and tenth vertical lines of hieroglyphs. These inscriptions read:—

On the right side of the box are one horizontal and twenty-five vertical lines of hieroglyphs. Between the fifth and sixth, the tenth and eleventh, the fifteenth and sixteenth, and the twentieth and twenty-first lines are vertical bands of inscription continued from the lid above and running down to the bottom of the box. In the panels thus formed are : firstly an inscription in five long vertical lines, and secondly figures of the King and Anubis. These inscriptions read :—

Vertical line of hieroglyphs, given on page XXXV, No. 4

FIGURE OF THE KING, STANDING.

Vertical line of hieroglyphs, given on page XXXV, No. 3.

FIGURE OF THE KING, STANDING.

Vertical line of hieroglyphs, given on page XXXV, No. 2.

FIGURE OF ANUBIS, STANDING.

Vertical line of hieroglyphs, given on page XXXV, No. 1.

FIGURE OF THE KING, STANDING.

On the left side of the box are one horizontal and twenty-five vertical lines of hieroglyphs. Between the fifth and sixth, the tenth and eleventh, the fifteenth and sixteenth, and the twentieth and twenty-first lines are vertical bands of inscriptions continued from the lid above and running down to the bottom of the box. In the panels thus formed are : firstly an inscription in five vertical lines divided in half by a figure of an 𓂀 , and secondly figures of the King and Anubis. These inscriptions read :—

FIGURE OF THE KING, STANDING.

Vertical line of hieroglyphs, given on page xxxvi, No. 8.

FIGURE OF THE KING, STANDING.

Vertical line of hieroglyphs, given on page xxxvi, No. 7.

FIGURE OF ANUBIS, STANDING.

Vertical line of hieroglyphs, given on page xxxvi, No. 6.

FIGURE OF THE KING, STANDING.

Vertical line of hieroglyphs, given on page xxxvi, No. 5.

Standing figure of Isis with arms upraised and wearing the 𓊗–sign upon her head.

On the square end of the box are one horizontal and fourteen vertical lines of hieroglyphs, with a standing figure of Isis with arms upraised and wearing the 𓊗–sign upon her head, in the centre, between the seventh and eighth vertical lines of hieroglyphs. These inscriptions read:—

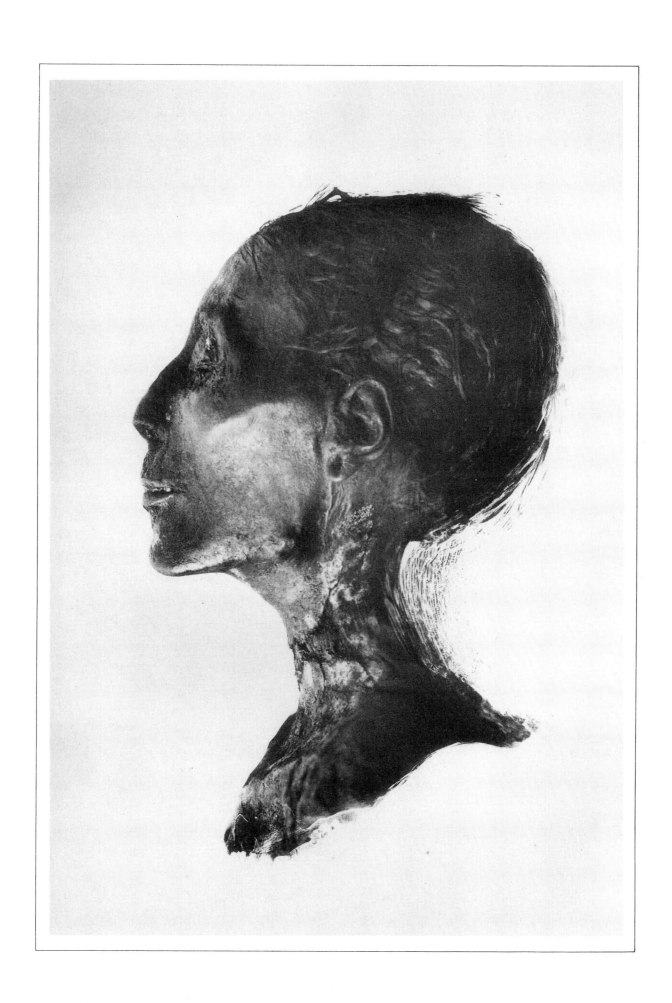

HEAD OF THOUTMŌSIS IV.

THE PHYSICAL CHARACTERS OF THE MUMMY OF THOUTMÔSIS IV,

BY

G. ELLIOT SMITH.

THE body is that of a young, clean-shaven, effeminate, and extremely emaciated man, 5 feet 6 inches in height. It shows no sign of any ante-mortem injury; but both feet have been broken off at some time long after the body was embalmed, and the right leg was broken off at the knee-joint. A transverse abrasion on the front of the neck may have been produced at the same time as these other injuries. The body is so emaciated that all the ribs stand out as prominent ridges. The thorax shows a slight flattening in the region of the third right rib in front, but there is no evidence to show that this was the result of disease.

For purposes of embalming, the abdominal wall had been removed in the whole of the left iliac and part of the left hypogastric regions, leaving a large triangular opening measuring 11·5 cm. transversely, 10 cm. in the vertical direction, and 14 cm. along the third margin, which was parallel to and just above Poupart's ligament. The whole abdomino-thoracic cavity was tightly packed with cloth saturated with resinous embalming-material, which formed a very hard solid mass. A large mass of cloth was stuffed into the mouth of the opening in the abdominal wall. There was no trace of any of the viscera in the embalming-material, which filled up the whole body-cavity. It was also impossible to determine the cause of a large opacity, about the size of a fist, which made its appearance in the left side of the thorax in a skiagraph.

The body was lying in a fully-extended, prone position. The shoulders were slightly raised : the upper arms were placed vertically, and the forearms were crossed on the front of the chest, the right forearm being in front of the left. The hands were flexed in such a manner that they must (at the time of embalming) have been grasping vertical rods, each about 1·5 cm. in diameter.

The skin is very dark and discoloured, so that it is not possible to form any accurate idea of its original colour.

The head has a very effeminate appearance, especially when seen in profile. The face is long, narrow, and ovoid: the chin is narrow, prominent, and somewhat pointed. The forehead has a most pronounced slope, and there is no projection in the region of the glabella or the superciliary ridges. There is no depression at the nasion, the line of the forehead (when viewed in profile) passing straight down into continuity with the anterior margin of the nose. The nose is relatively small, narrow, slightly aquiline, and delicately moulded. The lower margin of the septum nasi is very oblique.

Practically no distortion of the nose and face has occurred in the process of embalming: the nasal apertures are symmetrical and not dilated. The lateral cartilages are pushed outward to a slight extent beyond the nasal bones, and there is a pronounced median sagittal groove extending along the whole of the cartilaginous part of the nose.

The ears are small and well moulded: the lobules are fixed and, like those of Rameses II, have large perforations, so that each lobule is converted into a rounded cord. The lips are thin.

In norma verticalis the head presents the form called "beloides aegyptiacus" by Sergi. The cephalic (breadth-length) index is 77·7, so that it falls into the mesaticephalic group.

The skin of the forehead is transversely wrinkled just in front of the hair, but from its appearance it is a post-mortem change.

The hair of the head is slightly wavy, is about 16 cm. long, and is of a dark reddish-brown (henna-colour) tint: in front it has the appearance of having been parted slightly to the left of the middle line, but elsewhere it is matted together in a tangle of thick locks, which hang obliquely downward and backward on the side of the head. The colour of the hair is different to the dark brown tint which is usually found in the people of Egypt. Microscopic examination probably explains the meaning of this by revealing a mass of dark reddish foreign matter (? embalming material or possibly henna) studding the surface of the hair.

The eyebrows are moderately thick: they extend inward as a thinner group of hairs which meet across the middle line.

The moustache and beard were closely shaved. It was possible to recognise the cut ends of a fairly thick moustache, which was most dense just above the angles of the mouth. There was also evidence of a thick patch of hair in front of and co-extensive with the auditory pinna, but over the masseteric and buccal regions the hair was very scanty. On the lower lip and the polished anterior surface of the chin it was impossible to find more than a very few scattered hairs; but on the under surface of the chin a small group of scattered hairs was visible. Neither on the neck, nor on the limbs and thorax could any hair be detected; and even on the pubic area it was impossible to find any certain traces of hair.

All parts of the surface of the body, including the somewhat diminutive genital organs, were well preserved. Circumcision seems to have been performed.

Eight of the upper teeth were visible after a small quantity of resinous embalming material had been removed. They were white, unworn, and in excellent condition. None of the lower teeth were visible, being hidden by the lower lip. The upper incisors were obliquely set, so that they must have projected over the corresponding lower teeth.

The delicate hands were extremely emaciated: this fact, together with the great length of the finger nails, made the fingers seem much longer and slenderer than they really were. The finger nails were long and narrow, and had not been trimmed for three or four weeks before death.

As the determination of the age of Thoutmôsis IV at the time of his death would afford evidence of considerable value to historians, a careful search was made for some indications on which to base an estimation. As the body had every appearance of being that of a young man, it seemed possible that an examination of the bony epiphyses might enable us to determine the age. Dr. Herbert Milton kindly enabled us to examine the skeleton by means of his Röntgen-ray apparatus. It was in this way demonstrated that the epiphyses of the long bones were fully-joined, and a direct examination of the ends of the tibia in the damaged right leg showed the perfect union of its epiphyses. Thus the man must have been 20 years of age at least, and probably more than 24 years. On the other hand, the examination of the crest of the ilium (both by the Röntgen rays and directly in the embalming-incision) showed that the epiphyses of the crest of the ilium was not fully joined. So that the body is most probably that of a man of not more than 25 years. And as the union of the epiphyses of the other bones seems to prove that the body is more than 24 years old, we cannot be far from the truth in assigning the age of 25 years to Thoutmôsis IV at the time of his death.

MEASUREMENTS OF THE BODY.

	m.
Height of body	1·646
Height to the chin	1·452
Height of shoulders	1·410
Height of suprasternal notch	1·340
Height of umbilicus	1·040

	mm.
Maximum length of head (glabella to inion) ...	184
Maximum breadth of head	143
Minimum frontal breadth	95
Circumference of head	537
Length of nose	55
Breadth of nose	29
Vertical projections—	
Vertex to root of nose	77
Vertex to mouth	145
Vertex to chin	185
Vertex to tragus	111
Chin to glabella	121
Upper lip	83·5
Biauricular breadth	130
Bizygomatic breadth...	130
Diameters of face—	
External orbital breadth	97·5
Internal orbital breadth (roughly)	28·5
Bigonial breadth	102
Ear (pinna)—	
Maximum length ... ... *r.* 52 mm. ; *l.*	52
Maximum breadth ... ... *r.* 24 mm. ; *l.*	30
(Left ear better preserved.)	
Biorbito-nasal arc	113
Breadth of shoulders	382
Breadth of hips	270
Breadth of iliac crests	265
Breadth between ant. iliac spine	200
Axial length of right tibia	376

	mm.
Length of right tibia with malleolus	386
Length from prominence of great trochanter to external condyle (right femur)	440
Right arm—	
Length from tip of acromion to external condyle of humerus	358
Length from tip of acromion to olecranon ...	363·5
Length from external condyle to radial styloid	
Length of thumb (from tubercle of scaphoid) ...	120
Length of middle finger (from lower end of radius)	210
Breadth of carpus	46
Breadth of the distal end of the metacarpus (four fingers)	53
Length of foot	222
Maximum breadth of foot	67

First and second toes of the same length.

PLATE II.

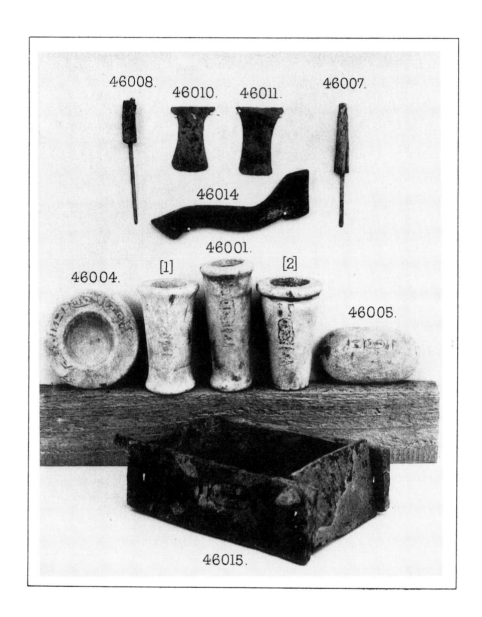

FOUNDATION DEPOSITS.

CATALOGUE OF THE ANTIQUITIES

FOUND IN

THE TOMB OF THOUTMÔSIS IV,

BY

HOWARD CARTER AND PERCY E. NEWBERRY.

—ᵒᵒ⟐ᵒᵒ—

1. THE FOUNDATION DEPOSITS.

— **Vase** [1].—Arragonite.—Height 0 m ·08.—Diameter of top 0 m ·05 ; diameter across base 0 m ·04.—Plan, *f.d.*—Plate II. [1].

⦚–shaped vase, with a vertical line of hieroglyphs incised upon its side giving the prenomen of Thoutmôsis IV : ⦚⦚⦚⦚⦚.
[Davis Collection.]

— **Vase** [2].—Arragonite.—Height 0 m ·08.—Diameter of top 0 m ·05 ; diameter across base 0 m ·03.—Plan, *f.d.*—Plate II. [2].

⦚–shaped vase, bearing a similar inscription to that of No. [1].
[Davis Collection.]

46001. **Vase** [3]. Arragonite.—Height 0 m ·095.—Diameter of top 0 m ·04 ; diameter across base 0 m ·03.—Plan, *f.d.*—Plate II.

⦚–shaped vase, with a vertical line of hieroglyphs incised upon its side ⦚⦚⦚⦚⦚.

46002. **Vase** [4].—Arragonite.—Height 0 m ·065.—Diameter of top 0 m ·04 ; diameter across base 0 m ·03.—Plan, *f.d.*

⦚–shaped vase, bearing a similar inscription to that of No. 46001.

Catal. du Musée, n. 46001.

1

46003.   Vase [5].—Arragonite.—Height 0 m ·065.—Diameter of top 0 m ·05 ; diameter across base 0 m ·035.—Plan, *f.d.*

〖–shaped vase, bearing a similar inscription to that of No. 46001.

46004.   Saucer [6].—Arragonite.—Maximum diameter 0 m ·08.—Depth 0 m ·02. Plan, *f.d.*—Plate II.

A shallow ▽-shaped saucer, with an incised inscription on one side of its rim : [hieroglyphs]. Beneath this inscription can be read another : [hieroglyphs], showing that the vase had been originally intended for the tomb of Hatshopsouît, and that it was afterwards re-used by Thoutmôsis IV.

—   **Saucer** [7].—Arragonite.—Maximum diameter 0 m ·06.—Depth 0 m ·02. —Plan, *f.d.*

A shallow ▽-shaped saucer, with a roughly-incised inscription on its rim : [hieroglyphs].

[Davis Collection.]

—   **Saucer** [8].—Arragonite.—Maximum diameter 0 m ·05.—Depth 0 m ·02. —Plan, *f.d.*

A shallow ▽-shaped saucer, bearing a similar inscription to that of No. [7].

[Davis Collection.]

46005.   Pebble [9].—Arragonite.—Length 0 m ·08.—Breadth 0 m ·05.— Plan, *f.d.*—Plate II.

An oval-shaped pebble, bearing the following inscription written upon it in black ink : [hieroglyphs].

46006.   Pebble [10].—Arragonite.—Length 0 m ·08.—Breadth 0 m ·05.— Plan, *f.d.*

An oval-shaped pebble, bearing a similar inscription to that of No. 46005. The inscription is very faint.

46007.   Model Chisel [11].—Bronze blade with wooden handle.—Length of blade 0 m ·04 ; length of handle 0 m ·05.—Plan, *f.d.*—Plate II.

A small model chisel, with flat bronze blade and wooden handle of round section.

46008. Model Chisel [12].—Bronze blade with wooden handle.—Length of blade 0 m ·06 ; length of handle 0 m ·03.—Plan, *f.d.*—Plate II.

A small model chisel, with flat bronze blade and wooden handle of round section.

46009. Handle of a Model Chisel [13].—Wood.—Length 0 m ·14.— Plan, *f.d.*

Handle of a model chisel, with the following inscription written upon it in black ink :

46010. Model Axe blade [14].—Bronze.—Length 0 m ·05.—Maximum breadth 0 m ·04.—Plan, *f.d.*—Plate II.

Model axe blade, in bronze, with the following inscription incised upon it :

46011. Model Axe blade [15].—Bronze.—Length 0 m ·05.—Maximum breadth 0 m ·04.—Plan, *f.d.*—Plate II.

Model axe blade, in bronze, similar to No. 46010, but without inscription.

46012. Model Axe blade [16].—Bronze.—Length 0 m ·05.—Maximum breadth 0 m ·04.—Plan, *f.d.*

Model axe blade, in bronze, similar to No. 46010, but without inscription.

46013. Blade of a Model Adze [17].—Bronze.—Length 0 m ·06.—Breadth 0 m ·02.—Plan, *f.d.*

Blade for model adze, uninscribed.

46014. Handle of a Model Adze [18].—Wood.—Length 0 m ·13.—Plan, *f.d.*— Plate II.

Handle of a model adze, with the following inscription incised upon it :

46015. Model Brick-Mould [19].—Wood.—Length 0 m ·135.—Breadth 0 m ·065.—Plan, *f.d.*—Plate II.

Model brick-mould, composed of four strips of wood dovetailed together. Upon one side is roughly incised the following inscription :

1.

46016.   Model Brick-Mould [20].—Wood.—Length 0 m ·17.—Breadth 0 m ·08. Plan, *f.d.*

Model brick-mould, similar to No. 46015.

46017.   Finger Ring [21].—Blue glazed faïence.—Diameter 0 m ·017.— Plan, *f.d.*

A plain blue glazed faïence finger-ring, without bezel.

46018.   Cartouche-shaped Plaque [22].—Blue glazed faïence.—Length 0 m ·02.—Plan, *f.d.*

A small cartouche-shaped plaque, bearing the prenomen of Thouthmôsis IV :

46019.   Cartouche-shaped Plaque [23].—Blue glazed faïence.—Length 0 m ·02.—Plan, *f.d.*

A small cartouche-shaped plaque, similar to No. 46018.

46020.   Plaque [24].—Blue glazed faïence.—Length 0 m ·02.—Width 0 m ·015. —Plan, *f.d.*

A small plaque, with a kneeling ibex modelled in relief upon its upper surface.

46021.   Plaque [25].—Blue glazed faïence.—Length 0 m ·02.—Plan, *f.d.*

A small plaque in the shape of a lion's head. Flat below ; modelled in relief upon its upper surface.

46022.   Plaque [26].—Blue glazed faïence.—Length 0 m ·02.—Plan, *f.d.*

A small plaque in the shape of a calf's head. Flat below ; modelled in relief upon its upper surface.

46023.   Plaque [27].—Blue glazed faïence.—Length 0 m ·02.—Plan, *f.d.*

A small plaque, similar to No. 46022.

46024.   Plaque [28].—Blue glazed faïence.—Length 0 m ·02.—Plan, *f.d.*

A small plaque, in the shape of a human hand ; modelled in relief upon its upper surface, flat below.

46025.   Plaque [29].—Blue glazed faïence.—Length 0 m ·02.—Plan, *f.d.*

A small plaque, similar to No. 46024.

46026. **Plaque** [30].—Blue glazed faïence.—Length 0 m ·02.—Plan, *f.d.*

A small plaque, similar to No. 46024.

46027. **Plaque** [31].—Blue glazed faïence.—Length 0 m ·02.—Plan, *f.d.*

A small plaque, similar to No. 46024.

46028. **Plaque** [32].—Blue glazed faïence.—Length 0 m ·025.—Plan, *f.d.*

A small plaque, having on its upper surface a flying pin-tailed duck modelled in relief; flat below.

46029. **Plaque** [33].—Blue glazed faïence.—Length 0 m ·025.—Plan, *f.d.*

A small plaque, similar to No. 46028.

46030. **Plaque** [34].—Blue glazed faïence.—Length 0 m ·023.—Plan, *f.d.*

A small plaque, in the shape of a bivalve shell; slightly rounded above, flat below.

46031. **Plaque** [35].—Blue glazed faïence.—Length 0 m ·023.—Plan, *f.d.*

A small plaque, similar to No. 46030.

46032. **Plaque** [36].—Blue glazed faïence.—Length 0 m ·023.—Plan, *f.d.*

A small plaque, similar to No. 46030.

46033. **Plaque** [37].—Blue glazed faïence.—Length 0 m ·025.—Plan, *f.d.*

A small plaque, in the shape of a lotus-flower; modelled in low relief above, flat below.

46034. **Plaque** [38].—Blue glazed faïence.—Height 0 m ·025.—Plan, *f.d.*

A small plaque, similar to No. 46030.

46035. **Plaque** [39].—Blue glazed faïence.—Height 0 m ·015.—Plan, *f.d.*

A small oblong plaque; rounded above, flat below.

2. THE CANOPIC JARS AND THEIR BOX.

Canopic Jar [1].—Limestone.—Height 0 m ·395.—Maximum diameter
0 m ·17.—Chamber 4.—Plate III [1].

Lid of jar, carved in the form of a human head wearing a full wig. The face is
well modelled, and the eyebrows, eyelashes and irides of the eyes are painted
in black.

Jar, of the usual rounded form, hollowed out inside and with a vertical column of
hieroglyphs running down the front. The hieroglyphs are incised, coloured blue,
and divided from the rest of the jar by vertical incised lines, also coloured blue.
The inscription reads :

The lid is perfect ; the jar itself is broken into five pieces.

TECHNIQUE, fair.

[Davis Collection.]

46036.   Canopic Jar [2].—Limestone.—Height 0 m ·39.—Maximum diameter
0 m ·18.—Chamber 4.

Lid of jar, similar to that of the preceding [No. 1].

Jar, similar to that of the preceding, but with the following inscription incised upon it :

The lid is perfect ; the jar itself is broken into several pieces.

TECHNIQUE, fair.

46037.   Canopic Jar of the Prince Amenemhat [3].—Limestone.—Height
0 m ·35.—Maximum diameter 0 m ·15.—Chamber 4.—Plate III.

Lid of jar, carved in the form of a human head wearing a full wig and " false
beard, the latter painted blue. The hair of the wig is emphasised by incised
parallel vertical lines. The face is well-modelled, and the eyebrows, eyelashes and
irides of the eyes are painted in black.

Jar, of the usual rounded form, hollowed out in the inside and with an inscription of
four vertical lines of hieroglyphs, divided from the rest of the jar by vertical and
horizontal incised lines, forming a panel. The hieroglyphs are incised and coloured
blue. The inscription reads :

The lid is perfect ; the jar itself is broken into several pieces.

TECHNIQUE, good.

PLATE III.

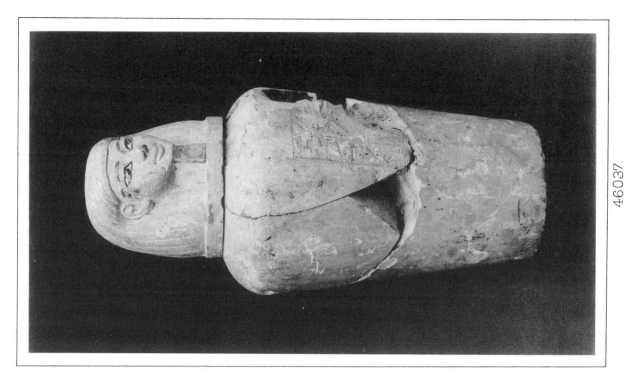

46037.

CANOPIC JARS.

[1]

46038. Canopic Jar of the Prince Amenemhat [4].—Limestone.—Height 0 m ·375.—Maximum diameter 0 m ·16.—Chamber 4.

Lid of jar, similar to that of the preceding No. 46037.

Jar, similar to that of the preceding No. 46037, but with the following inscription incised upon it:

(1) [hieroglyphs] (2) [hieroglyphs] (3) [hieroglyphs] (4) [hieroglyphs]

The lid is perfect; the jar itself is broken into several pieces.

TECHNIQUE, good.

— Canopic Jar of the Prince Amenemhat [5].—Limestone.—Height 0 m ·38.—Maximum diameter 0 m ·18.—Chamber 4.

Lid of jar, similar to that of No. 46037.

Jar, similar to that of No. 46037, but with the following inscription incised upon it:

(1) [hieroglyphs] (2) [hieroglyphs] (3) [hieroglyphs] (4) [hieroglyphs]

The lid is perfect; the jar is broken into several pieces.

TECHNIQUE, good.

[Davis Collection.]

46039. Canopic Jar of the Prince Amenemhat [6].—Limestone.—Height 0 m ·38.—Maximum diameter 0 m ·155.—Chamber 4.

Lid of jar, similar to that of No. 3.

Jar, similar to that of No. 3, but with the following inscription incised upon it:

(1) [hieroglyphs] (2) [hieroglyphs] (3) [hieroglyphs] (4) [hieroglyphs]

The lid is perfect; the jar is broken into several pieces.

TECHNIQUE, good.

46040. Fragments of Canopic Jars of the Princess Thent-amen [7].— Arragonite.—Chamber 4.

Several small pieces of the lids of these jars were found; they were human-headed, and beautifully sculptured. A piece of the body of one of these jars bears the following vertical line of hieroglyphs, incised but not coloured: [hieroglyphs]

[hieroglyphs].

TECHNIQUE, very good.

46041. Fragments of a box for Canopic Jars [8].—Arragonite.—
Chamber 4.

A large number of small fragments of an alabaster (arragonite) box for canopic jars
was found, and some of these were inscribed. Unfortunately, these pieces were
too fragmentary to permit of their being fitted together, but from them we gain
sufficient evidence to assume that the box was similar in shape to the one found
in the tomb of Amenôphis II (see Daressy, *Fouilles de la vallée des rois*, in *Catalogue
général des Antiquités Égyptiennes de musée du Caire*, No. 5029, Pl. L).

PLATE IV.

46042.

46044.

MAGICAL FIGURES.

3. THE FOUR MAGICAL FIGURES.

46042. The Magical Figure of the Northern Wall [1].—Painted Wood [1] with pedestal of sun-baked clay.—Height of figure 0 m ·185.— Dimensions of pedestal.—Height 0 m ·05.—Length 0 m ·157.— Width 0 m ·072.—Chamber 4.—Plate IV.

Figure carved in the form of a human mummy swathed in a winding sheet. The face is beautifully modelled, and painted yellow, with eyebrows and eyelashes emphasized by black lines, the eyes by white pupils and black irides. Upon the head is a long wig coloured black, and the winding sheet over the body is painted white. The figure is represented standing, and is fixed by a wooden peg into the

Pedestal of sun-baked clay. On the front of the pedestal is painted in white the word ⟨hieroglyph⟩, while on the upper surface, immediately before the feet of the figure, are six horizontal lines of hieroglyphs giving the magical text from Chapter CLI (*d*) of the *Book of the Dead*:—

TECHNIQUE, very good.

46043. Pedestal of the Magical Flame [2] **of the Southern Wall** [2].— Sun-baked clay. — Height 0 m ·03. — Length 0 m ·16.—Width 0 m ·085.—Chamber 4.

Pedestal of sun-baked clay. On the front of it is painted in white the word ⟨hieroglyph⟩, while on its upper surface, immediately before a hole in which the magical flame was fixed, are six horizontal lines of hieroglyphs, giving the following text from Chapter CLI (*f*) of the *Book of the Dead*:—

[1] Apparently of date-palm wood, thus agreeing with the rubric given in the papyri, which also states that the figure is to be seven fingers high. See Naville, in the *Proceedings of the Society of Biblical Archæology*, Vol. XXV, p. 108.

[2] According to the rubric given in the papyri, the flame was a torch made of *uaa*-reeds.

46044. The Magical Jackal of the Eastern Wall [3].—Sun-baked clay painted.—Height of figure to tip of ear 0 m ·14.—Dimensions of pedestal.—Height 0 m ·042.—Length 0 m ·285.—Width 0 m ·085 Chamber 4. (Found in niche in left-hand end column untouched.) —Plate IV.

The Figure of the jackal is represented lying down, with its forelegs stretched in front, head and ears erect, and tail curled round its right side. The modelling of the animal is exquisite, and the figure appears to have been painted grey, with pupils of the eyes white and irides black. It is modelled directly on the top of the

Pedestal, which has been broken into three pieces.[1] On the front of it is painted in white the word ∱⌒⌒, and immediately before the paws of the jackal were six horizontal lines of hieroglyphs painted in white, giving the magical text from Chapter CLI (*g*) of the *Book of the Dead*. Of this text only the following hieroglyphs have been preserved :—

TECHNIQUE, very fine.

46045. Pedestal of the Magical *Ded*[2] of the Western Wall [4].—Sun-baked clay.—Height 0 m ·038.—Length 0 m ·158.—Width 0 m ·073. Chamber 4.

Pedestal of sun-baked clay. On the front of it is painted in white the word ∱⌒⌒, while on its upper surface, immediately before the holes in which the magical *Ded* was fixed, are eight horizontal lines of hieroglyphs painted in white, giving the following text from Chapter CLI (*e*) of the *Book of the Dead* :—

---

[1] The front piece is not shown in the photograph given in Plate VIII, 3.

[2] According to the rubric given in the papyri, this *Ded* had to be made of "crystal," the branches of which were to be of "gold." This would have made it a valuable object, and probably accounts for its having disappeared from the tomb.

PLATE V.

46049.

46066.

46046.

46069.

46055.

46065.

46047.

WOODEN STATUETTES.

4. THE WOODEN FIGURES.

46046. Statuette [1].—Wood coated with bitumen.—Height 0 m ·60.— Chamber 4.—Plate V.

Statuette of the king wearing the crown of Lower Egypt, a false beard, and the *shenti* loin-cloth suspended by a broad belt. The figure is shown slightly bending forward, the left foot is flat upon the ground and the right leg is stretched out behind, the toes only being on the ground. The left arm is stretched out in front of the figure as if in the attitude of holding an enemy by the hair, while the right arm is raised as if in the act of striking with a mace or battle-axe.

Badly mutilated. The left arm is wanting below the elbow, the left leg below the knee. The right leg is broken across about half way down the shin, but the lower piece is not shown in the photograph (Plate V).

The base on which the statuette was standing is lost.

46047. Statuette [2].—Wood coated with bitumen.—Height 0 m ·61.— Chamber 4.—Plate V.

Statuette of the king wearing the crown of Upper Egypt, and clad in a short, plain loin-cloth. The figure is represented in the attitude of walking, with the left leg thrust forward. The right arm hangs down at the side ; the left is raised from the elbow as if the hand held a sceptre.

Badly mutilated. The face is broken away and a piece of the left leg is wanting.

The base on which the statuette was standing is lost.

46048. Statuette [3].—Wood coated with bitumen.—Height 0 m ·61.— Found in the well.

Statuette of the king wearing the crown of Lower Egypt, a false beard, and the *shenti* garment. The figure is represented in the attitude of walking, with the left leg thrust forward. The right arm hangs down at the side ; the left is raised from the elbow as if a sceptre was held in the hand.

Badly mutilated. The left leg is broken across the middle of the shin, and the right leg is missing below the knee.

The base on which the statuette was standing is lost.

46049. Statuette [4].—Wood coated with bitumen.—Height of figure to forehead 0 m ·29.—Chamber 4.—Plate V.

Statuette of the king wearing the same insignia and represented in the same attitude as No. 46048.

Badly mutilated. The left arm is wanting from the elbow ; the left side of the face is broken away, and the top of the crown of Lower Egypt is broken and wanting.

The wooden pedestal is preserved; its dimensions are: Height 0 m ·03, breadth 0 m ·065, length 0 m ·185.

2.

46050.   **Statuette** [5].—Wood coated with bitumen.—Height of figure to forehead 0 m ·295.—Chamber 4.

Statuette of the king represented in the same attitude as No. 46048, but wearing the crown of Upper Egypt.

Badly mutilated.   The left arm is missing from the elbow, and the left foot is wanting.

One side of the wooden pedestal is preserved.   The dimensions are : Height 0 m ·03, length 0 m ·185.

46051.   **Two arms of a Statuette** [6].—Wood coated with bitumen.—Length of arm 0 m ·235.—Chamber 4.

Two arms from a standing statuette of the king.   The right arm is shown as if it had been hanging down at the side of the figure.   The left arm is raised as if the hand held a sceptre.

In fair preservation.

46052.   **Fragments of the left arm of a Statuette** [7].—Wood coated with bitumen.—Chamber 4.

Fragments of the left arm of a statuette of the king, similar to No. 46051, and of about the same proportions.   The arm is raised from the elbow as if the hand had been holding a sceptre.

46053.   **Fragments of a Statuette** [8].—Wood coated with bitumen.—Length of face from forehead to chin 0 m ·08.—Chamber 4.

Seven fragments of the face, arms and feet of a statuette of the king.   He is shown wearing a linen (?) head-dress wrapped tightly across the forehead and falling behind the ears on to the shoulders.   To the chin was attached a false beard.

Badly mutilated.

46054.   **Fragments of a Statuette** [9].—Wood coated with bitumen.—Length of thumb 0 m ·10.—Chamber 4.

Four fragments of the hand and feet of a large statuette of the king.

TECHNIQUE, very fine.

46055.   **Statuette** [10].—Wood coated with bitumen.—Height 0 m ·54.—Chamber 4.—Plate V.

Statuette of the king, represented in the form of a mummy wearing a long wig falling over the shoulders and the breast.   On the top of the head is a narrow hole, doubtless for fixing on the double-feathered crown.

Badly mutilated.   The face is wanting; the body has been chipped in places and a piece broken away from the left side.   The feet also are missing.

TECHNIQUE, poor.

— **Statuette** [11].—Wood coated with bitumen.—Height 0 m ·54.—
Found in débris outside the tomb.

Statuette of the king, similar to No. 46055.

Badly mutilated. Face and left side partly decayed away.

[Davis Collection.]

46056. Statuette [12].—Wood coated with bitumen.—Height 0 m ·56.—
Chamber 4.

Statuette of the king, similar to No. 46055.

Badly mutilated. Face wanting.

46057. Face of a Statuette [13].—Wood coated with bitumen.—Chamber 4.

Face of a statuette, with eyes painted white, pupils black and eyebrows green.
From the size of the face, the dimensions of the statuette must have been similar
to No. 46055.

46058. Statuette [14].—Wood coated with bitumen.—Height 0 m ·35.—
Chamber A.

Statuette, in the form of a mummy, wearing the royal head-dress with twisted
tail of hair at the back of the head. Over the forehead are the remains of a
gilt uræus, and down the front of the figure is a vertical column of incised
hieroglyphs giving the prenomen of Thoutmôsis IV :

Mutilated. Feet wanting.

46059. Statuette [15].—Wood coated with bitumen.—Height from chin to
bottom of feet 0 m ·285.—Chamber 4.

Statuette, in the form of a royal mummy. Down the front of the figure is a
vertical column of incised hieroglyphs giving the prenomen of Thoutmôsis IV :

Mutilated. Head, crown and feet wanting.

46060. Statuette [16].—Wood coated with bitumen.—Height 0 m ·28.—
Chamber 4.

Statuette, in the form of a mummy, similar to No. 46058, but inscribed down the
front of the figure with a vertical column of incised hieroglyphs reading

Badly mutilated. Face and feet wanting.

46061.   Statuette [17].—Wood coated with bitumen.—Height 0 m ·315.—
    Chamber 4.

Statuette, in the form of a mummy, wearing a full wig ending behind in a broad
row of plaits. Over the forehead are the remains of a gilt uræus, and down the
front of the figure are traces of an incised inscription giving the prenomen of
Thoutmôsis IV.

Mutilated. Right arm broken away.

46062.   Statuette [18].—Wood coated with bitumen.—Height 0 m ·28.—
    Chamber 4.

Statuette, in the form of a mummy, similar to No. 46061, but with a necklace in
yellow painted *over* the bitumen, and with eyes and eyebrows outlined in yellow.

In fair preservation.

46063.   Statuette [19].—Wood coated with bitumen.—Length of face from
    forehead to chin 0 m ·035.—Chamber 4.

Statuette, similar to No. 46058, with traces of an incised inscription down the front
of the figure: .

Mutilated. The legs and feet are wanting below the knees.

46064.   Statuette [20].—Wood coated with bitumen.—Height 0 m ·295.—
    Found in the sarcophagus.

Statuette, in the form of a mummy, wearing a close-fitting cap or short wig. Down
the front of the figure is an incised inscription beginning: .

Badly mutilated. The face and right side of the head are wanting; the right arm,
a piece of the left leg, and both feet are missing.

46065.   Statuette [21].—Wood coated with bitumen.—Height 0 m ·56 from
    the tip of ear to sole of feet.—Chamber 4.—Plate V.

Statuette of the goddess Sekhemet. She is represented with lion head, wearing long
wig, and seated on a solid wooden chair of the usual -type.

Mutilated. Base or pedestal wanting.

Technique, fair.

46066. Panther [22].—Wood coated with bitumen.—Length from tip of nose to rump 1 m ·06.—Chamber 4.—Plate V.

> Statuette, carved to represent a prowling panther, with two wooden pegs projecting from the back, and presumably belonging to a throne or some other piece of furniture.

> Mutilated. The left fore-leg, right hind-leg and part of tail are wanting. Base or pedestal missing.

> TECHNIQUE, very fine.

46067. Head of a Bird [23].—Wood coated with bitumen.—Length from tip of beak to back of head 0 m ·105.—Chamber 4.

> Head of a bird of uncertain species.

46068. Goose [24].—Wood coated with bitumen.—Length from tip of tail to breast 0 m ·50.—Found in the sarcophagus.

> Model of a goose, with curved neck.

> Mutilated. Broken into three pieces. Legs and part of neck wanting.

> TECHNIQUE, fair.

46069. Head of a Cow [25].—Wood painted yellow.—Height 0 m ·42.—Chamber 4.—Found beneath sarcophagus lid.—Plate V.

> Head of a cow, carved in wood and painted yellow.

> Mutilated. The horns, which were perhaps of metal, are wanting, and both eyes have been chipped out, probably in order to remove some metal inlay.

> TECHNIQUE, good.

5. STONE VASES.

46070.   Fragments of a Vase [1].—Diorite.—Maximum diameter 0 m ·20.— Chamber 4.

Two fragments of the lower part of a ⌷-shaped vase.   Uninscribed.

46071.   Fragments of a Vase [2].—Diorite.—Maximum diameter 0 m ·21 ; diameter across mouth 0 m ·15.—Chamber 4.

Fragments of a ⬡-shaped vase.   Inscribed on the bowl with the prenomen of Thoutmôsis IV written vertically : (⬡).

46072.   Fragments of a Vase [3].—Diorite.—Diameter across mouth 0 m ·09 ; maximum diameter 0 m ·135.—Chamber 4.

Fragments of a ⬡-shaped vase.   Inscribed on the bowl with the prenomen of Thoutmôsis IV written horizontally : (⬡) ⎮⎮.

46073.   Fragments of a Vase [4]. — Diorite. — Diameter across mouth 0 m ·135.—Chamber 4.

Fragments of a ⬡-shaped vase.   Inscribed on the neck with the prenomen of Thoutmôsis IV written vertically : ⎮⎮ (⬡).

46074.   Fragments of a Vase [5]. — Diorite. — Diameter across mouth 0 m ·09.—Chamber 4.

Fragments of a ⬡-shaped vase.   Inscribed on the bowl with the prenomen of Thoutmôsis IV written vertically : ⎮⎮ (⬡)

46075.   Fragments of a Vase [6].—Diorite.—Chamber 4.

Fragments of a flat-bottom vase of doubtful shape.

46076.   Fragment of a Vase [7].—Green stone.—Chamber 4.

Fragment of the round bowl of a vase of doubtful shape.

46077. Fragment of a Vase [8].—Diorite.—Diameter across mouth 0 m ·125. —Chamber 4.

Fragment of the upper part of a -shaped vase.

46078. Fragment of a Vase [9].—Diorite.—Diameter of base 0 m ·062.— Chamber 3.

Lower part of a _/-shaped vase.

46079. Fragments of a Vase [10].—Diorite.—Diameter of base 0 m ·09.— Chamber 4.

Two pieces of the base of a ⊖-shaped vase.

46080. Fragments of a Vase [11].—Crystalline limestone.—Diameter of bowl 0 m ·21.—Chamber 4.

Five fragments of a vase in crystalline limestone, with the prenomen of Thoutmôsis IV incised upon it: [hieroglyphs]. On the right-hand side of the cartouche the word [hieroglyphs] is written in black ink.

46081. Fragments of a Vase [12].—Crystalline limestone.—Diameter across mouth 0 m ·07.—Chamber 4.

Two fragments of the lip, neck and handle of a vase in crystalline limestone. The lip is thin and projects considerably over the neck, the upper part of which is ornamented by two modelled bands running round it. The handle is ribbed.

46082. Fragments of a Vase [13].—Arragonite.—Chamber 4.

Fragments of a vase inscribed with the prenomen of Thoutmôsis IV: [hieroglyphs] (incised vertically). On the right-hand side of the cartouche are the words: [hieroglyphs] written in black ink.

46083. Fragment of a Vase [14].—Arragonite.—Chamber 4.

Fragment of a vase, with the words [hieroglyphs] incised upon it. The word [hieroglyphs] is written in black ink near the incised signs.

46084. Fragment of a Vase [15].—Arragonite.—Chamber 4.

Fragment of a vase, with remains of a handle, and the word [hieroglyphs] written upon it in black ink.

46085.   Fragments of a Vase [16].—Arragonite.—Chamber 4.

Fragment of a vase, with the prenomen of Thoutmôsis IV incised upon it: ⬚ (written vertically).   On the right-hand side of the cartouche the letter ☐ is written in black ink.   (This latter inscription may be restored ⬚)

46086.   Fragment of a Vase [17].—Arragonite.—Chamber 4.

Fragment of a vase, with ⬚ incised upon it, and the words ⬚ written near it in black ink.

46087.   Fragment of a Vase [18].—Arragonite.—Chamber 4.

Fragment of a vase, inscribed with the prenomen and nomen of Amenôphis II: ⬚.   On the left of the cartouches is written in black ink the word ⬚.

46088.   Fragment of a Vase [19].—Arragonite.—Chamber 4.

Fragment of a vase, with the prenomen and nomen of Amenôphis II incised upon it: ⬚.   On the right of the cartouche is written in black ink the word ⬚.

46089.   Fragment of a Vase [20].—Arragonite.—Chamber 4.

Fragment of a vase, with the prenomen of Amenôphis II incised upon it: ⬚.

46090.   Fragment of a Vase [21].—Arragonite.—Chamber 4.

Fragment of a vase, with the following inscription incised upon it :—

⬚

46091.   Fragment of a Vase [22].—Arragonite.—Chamber 4.

Fragment of a vase, with the prenomen of Amenôphis II incised upon it: ⬚.

46092.   Fragment of a Vase [23].—Arragonite.—Chamber 4.

Fragment of a vase, with the prenomen and nomen of Thoutmôsis III incised upon it :

46093.   Fragment of a Vase [24].—Arragonite.—Chamber 4.

Fragment of a ⋎-shaped vase, with the prenomen of Thoutmôsis IV incised upon it :

46094.   Fragment of a Vase [25].—Arragonite.—Chamber 4.

Fragment of a vase, with the following inscription incised upon it :

[A large number of small and uninscribed fragments of arragonite vases were also found, but none of them could be fitted together.]

6. ARTICLES OF FURNITURE, ETC.

— **Panel from the side of a Throne** [1].—Cedar wood.—Maximum height 0 m ·25 ; minimum length 0 m ·22.—Chamber 4.—Plate VI [1 and 1a].

Panel from the side of a throne, with scenes and inscriptions carved on both surfaces in low relief.

Obverse. In the centre is a figure of Thoutmôsis IV facing ←, seated on a throne, which rests on the ⊕ sign. The upper part of the head of the king is broken away. The figure is shown clad in a pointed kilt, and around the neck is a broad necklace. In his right hand he holds the flail or fly-flap, in the left the ⌐-sceptre. Above him, in a cartouche, is his prenomen ⬭. Before him stands a figure of the lion-headed goddess ⬭ Urt-hekau, facing →, represented clad in a long, plain, tight-fitting garment, and wearing a long wig and broad necklace. Upon her head is the solar disc, with pendent uræus hanging down over the forehead. Her left arm is upraised, the hand spread before the king's face, as if in the attitude of blessing him. The right arm is bent from the elbow, so that the hand reaches up to the left breast, and in this hand she holds the ⬭-sign. Behind her is (1) a ⬭–sign reaching from the top to bottom of the panel, and (2), a vertical column of hieroglyphs, reading : ⬭ ⬭. Behind the king is a standing figure of the Ibis-headed god Tahuti, facing ←, wearing a short kilt, long wig, and broad necklace. In his right hand he holds out before him a ⬭–sign reaching from top to bottom of the panel, and in his left, which is raised up to his left breast, he holds the ⬭-sign. Above him is his name, ⬭.

Reverse. Thoutmôsis IV, as a human-headed lion, with hawk's wings, and tail upraised, facing →, treads beneath his feet the bodies of his fallen Asiatic enemies. The inscriptions in front and over the back of the sphinx record (1) the king's names, ⬭, (2) the name of the goddess Uazŷt, ⬭, (3) ⬭, and (4) ⬭, the last two inscriptions being descriptive of the scene.

PLATE VI.

[1]

[1A]

WOODEN PANEL.

PLATE VII.

[2]

[2A]

WOODEN PANEL.

TECHNIQUE : The panel is made of thin pieces of cedar wood dovetailed together and pinned with wooden pegs. The cutting of the figures and hieroglyphs is excellent.

PRESERVATION : Broken into five pieces and badly chipped in places.

[Davis Collection.]

— **Panel from the side of a Throne** [2].—Cedar wood.—Maximum height 0 m ·25 ; minimum height 0 m ·22.—Chamber 4.—Plate VII [2 and 2a].

Panel from the side of throne, with scenes and inscriptions carved on both surfaces in low relief.

Obverse. In the centre is a figure of Thoutmôsis IV, facing ➤➤→, seated on a throne, which rests on the [sign]-sign. Upon his head he wears the crown of Lower Egypt, with uræus over the forehead. To his chin is attached a false beard, around his neck is a broad necklace, and girding his loins is a short kilt, ornamented with parallel lines. In his right hand he holds a flail, in his left the [sign]-sceptre ; above him is his name, [hieroglyphs]. In front of him, facing ←◄◄, stands the lion-headed goddess [hieroglyphs] Urt-[hekau], represented in a long, plain, tight-fitting garment, and wearing a long wig and broad necklace. Upon her head is the solar disc, with pendent uræus hanging down over the forehead. Her right arm is upraised as if in the attitude of blessing the king. The left arm is bent from the elbow, so that the hand reaches up to the left breast, and in this hand she holds the [sign]-sign. Behind her was a [sign]-sign, reaching from the top to the bottom of the panel, but only the tip of this sign is preserved. Behind the king is a lotus-leaf-shaped fan, with papyrus-shaped handle and [sign]-ring at end ; below this is a vertical line of hieroglyphs, reading : [hieroglyphs]. A narrow strip of the panel is wanting, and then comes a figure of the ibis-headed god Tahuti, facing ➤➤→, wearing a short kilt ornamented with parallel lines, a long wig, and broad necklace. His left arm is thrust forward, and in his hand is a long wand reaching from top to bottom of the panel. The right arm is raised from the elbow to the breast, and in this hand he holds the [sign]-sign, while in the angle formed by the bending of the elbow he holds up a long [sign]-sign, which reaches from top to bottom of the panel.

Above him is the following inscription, written in two vertical lines: (1) [hieroglyphs], (2) [hieroglyphs]. Behind him is a vertical column of hieroglyphs, reading : [hieroglyphs].

Reverse. Thoutmôsis IV, as a human-headed lion, with hawk's wings, and tail upraised, facing ←◄◄, treads beneath his feet the bodies of his fallen Nubian enemies. Flying behind him is a hawk with wings outspread, and holding in its claws the ♀-sign, while below it is a lotus-petal-shaped fan held up vertically by two arms projecting from an ⸶-sign. The inscription on this side of the panel reads:

TECHNIQUE: the panel is made of thin pieces of cedar wood dovetailed together and pinned with wooden pegs. The cutting of the figures and hieroglyphs is excellent.

PRESERVATION: broken into thin pieces and badly chipped in places. A narrow strip is missing from the centre.

[Davis Collection.]

— Fragment of the handle of a Fan [3].—Cedar wood.—Found in débris near the entrance to the Tomb.

Fragment of the carved handle of a fan, with edges pierced with holes for the insertion of the quills of ostrich feathers. The two surfaces are carved with scenes in low relief.

Obverse. In the centre is the upper part of the cartouche [of Thoutmôsis IV] surmounted by a crown, consisting of the double feathers upon a ⊙-sign, and two spreading horns and uræi having ⊙-signs upon their heads. Of the cartouche only the ⊙-sign remains, while on either side of it are the hieroglyphs ⅂[𝄬] and ⋀[♀]. Beyond these two hieroglyphs were (1) on the right side, a seated (?) figure of the king, facing ←, wearing the royal wig, with twisted tail and uræus suspended over the forehead, and (2) on the left side a similar seated (?) figure, facing →, but with plain long wig and without uræus, and having the signs ⅂⅂ behind it. The rim of the handle is ornamented with the common "rectangle" pattern.

Reverse. In the centre was a cartouche surmounted by two horns and the double feathers, with, on the right of it, the signs ⅂⅃ and a flying hawk with wings outspread. The hawk has a ⊙-sign with uræus upon its head, and holds in its claws a ♀-ring. The rim is ornamented with the common "rectangle" pattern.

TECHNIQUE: finely carved in low relief.

PRESERVATION: badly mutilated.

[Davis Collection.]

46095. Lower part of the handle of a Fan [4].—Cedar wood.—Maximum breadth 0 m ·23.—Chamber 4.—Plate VIII.

Lower part of the handle of a fan, with edges pierced with holes for the insertion of the quills of ostrich feathers. The two surfaces carved in low relief.

PLATE VIII.

46095.

WOODEN FAN.

46096.

FRAGMENTS OF THRONE.

Obverse. Scene representing Thoutmôsis IV, facing ➤➤➤→, clad in a short kilt ornamented with parallel lines, and wearing a broad necklace, seated on a throne in a light papyrus canoe floating upon the water. The head of the king is broken away; the two hands are raised to a level with the breast, and hold (1) the right, a ⌐ sceptre, and (2) the left, a flail. Before the king are his titles and prenomen:

[hieroglyphs], and behind him his nomen: [hieroglyphs in cartouche]

[hieroglyphs]. The throne is of the usual [sign]-shape, and is ornamented with the [sign]-sign in the left-hand lower corner, and a scale pattern at the top and on the right-hand side. The papyrus canoe has two guiding oars supported by poles at the stern. The rim is ornamented with the common "rectangle" pattern.

Reverse. Similar to obverse, but scene faces ←➤➤➤.

TECHNIQUE: finely carved in low relief.

PRESERVATION: broken into three pieces; the whole of the upper part missing.

46096. Fragments of the back of a Throne [5].—Cedar wood coated with stucco.—Chamber 4.—Two fragments shown in Plate VIII.

Eleven fragments of the back of a throne (?), with ornamentation modelled in fine stucco.

ORNAMENTATION: *Obverse*. So far as the ornamentation of the back of this throne (?) can be made out from the fragments that remain, we see that it consisted of (1) in the centre a large [sign]-sign in a panel of scales (see Plate XII, 5), with the words [hieroglyphs] written around the lower part of the *sam*-sign. This panel is enclosed by (2) a border of (*a*) disconnected coils and (*b*) "rectangles," separated on both sides from the rest of the ornamentation by lines having horizontal lines cutting across them. Outside this is (3) a panel ornamented with beadwork designs enclosing alternately (*a*) above, the titles, prenomen and nomen of Thoutmôsis IV, and (*b*) below, flowers and other devices. Above this panel, and probably extending along the whole breadth of the back, was another panel, the ornamentation of which consisted of two uræi facing one another, and supporting in front of them the names of Thoutmôsis IV in cartouches. Between the first two coils of the uræi are lotus flowers and buds with rosettes below, and beyond them, over the tail of the snake, were the extended wings of a hawk or vulture.

Reverse. The ornamentation of the reverse consisted of horizontal and vertical incised lines arranged in a manner not now apparent.

TECHNIQUE: very good.

7. THE CHARIOT.

ALTHOUGH the wheels and several other parts of the chariot are missing, through its having been broken up and partially destroyed by the ancient plunderers of the tomb, the fragments that remain, and the representations of the king's war chariot in the scenes modelled on the

THE CHARIOT.

framework of the "body," give us sufficient evidence to presume that it was constructed and composed of the following parts :—

(1) The "body," consisting of a semicircular framework open at the back, and with a floor for the charioteer to stand on.

(2) The carriage proper, i.e., the axletree and the wheels.

(3) The pole.

The body of the chariot was supported by the pole, which rested on the axletree, and, to steady it, it was strapped on either side of the axletree by bands of leather. It was placed as far back as possible, so as to take the weight of the charioteer, and thus relieve the pole and yoke, which served as a balance and means of harnessing the horses. The butt of the pole was dovetailed into a socket at the back of the body, and firmly secured by leather thongs to the front part, and in order to prevent it slipping back, two straps were fixed into the rim and tied to the pole. The floor was made of leather meshwork, which, by its elasticity, answered the purpose of springs.

The axle and wheels were of wood; the latter were composed of eight spokes tired with metal, and secured to the axle by means of metal axle-pins.

The pole was of wood covered with leather. It was bent into an elbow at about one-fifth of its length from the end, and was supported by a wooden yoke.

FIG. 1.

The horses were yoked to the chariot by the following harness, made of leather, probably ornamented with leather bosses:—

(1) The breast-harness, with girth and yoke-saddle.

(2) The bridle, nose-strap, forehead-, three cheek-, and one neck-strap.

(3) The reins, fixed to the nose-strap and passed through a loop attached to the breast-harness and girth.

Catal. du Musee, n. 46001.

4

We believe that the command of the horses was obtained simply by the nose-strap, and not by a snaffle or bit. A whip of leather with wooden handle was used by the charioteer to drive the horses.

Attached to the "body" of the chariot were, on the outside, a bow-case and two quivers, and, on the inside, a leather pocket or pouch with embossed flap to cover it.

46097.   Body of the Chariot [1].—Wood coated with canvas, stucco, and fine linen.—Height 0 m ·86.—Width 0 m ·52.—Breadth 1 m ·03— Chamber 3.—Plate IX, 1 and 2.

Fig. 2.

The body of the chariot is composed of a wood framework and panelling, the latter being covered with a canvas base for stucco, which is modelled with scenes and ornamentations in very low relief. The scenes consist of four panels, two inside and two outside, divided by an exceedingly decorative and ornamental design.

Outside. In the centre (see figures 1 and 2) is the nomen of Thoutmôsis IV in a cartouche, surmounted by a Ra-sign and double ostrich feathers. In the space above is a lion-headed bird with wings opened, and holding in its claws two symbols of life; upon its head is the sun's disc, with the two pendent uræi. Before each uræus is a ☉-sign. Below the cartouche is represented the ⏛-sign (symbol of joining), and to this is bound, according to the ordinary Egyptian convention,

PLATE IX.

1.

View of Inside.

1ᴬ

View of Outside.

PLATE X.

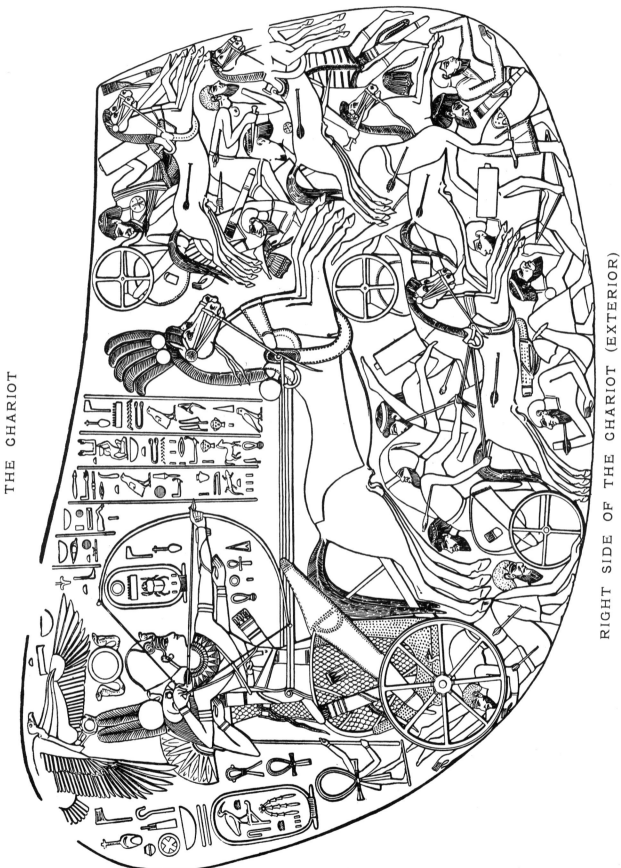

papyrus plants and lotus lilies.   Tied to the centre of the ⍦-sign on either side is
a row of kneeling Asiatic prisoners.

Off-side panel[1] (see Plate **X**).   Thoutmôsis IV, armed with bow and arrows, rides,
    unaccompanied save by Mentu, the god of war, into the midst of his enemy's chariot
    corps, which he throws into a state of the utmost confusion, and at the same time
    overthrows and sláys many of the charioteers.

Fɪɢ. 3.

The inscription explanatory of the scene is given in the five vertical lines above
the horses of the king's chariot, and reads:

---

[1] The great reduction of the Plates X, XI, and XII necessitated the small detail being left out.

4.

Hovering above the king is his protector, the goddess Nekhebyt, in the form of a vulture, holding in her talons the ♀–ring. Thoutmôsis IV is represented standing in his chariot, and is in the act of shooting an arrow from a bow; at the same time he guides his horses with the reins tied round his body. Behind him stands the hawk-headed god Mentu, wearing on his head the sun's disc, two feathers, and uræus. He guides the king's hands, and assures the accuracy of the monarch's aim. The king wears the war helmet, with uræus in front; around his neck are two

Fig. 4.

strings of beads with decorative border. He is clad in a loin-cloth, which is supported by a broad belt, and his torso is swathed with leathern or cloth bands. He wears armlets on either arm, a leathern gauntlet on his forearm, and a bracelet on his right wrist. Slung over his shoulders are two quivers full of arrows. The chariot, which is of simpler decoration than the original, bears a quiver and bow case, and is drawn by two horses richly caparisoned, and wearing ostrich feathers upon their heads. (For details of horses, see fig. 3.) The enemy which he is in

PLATE XI.

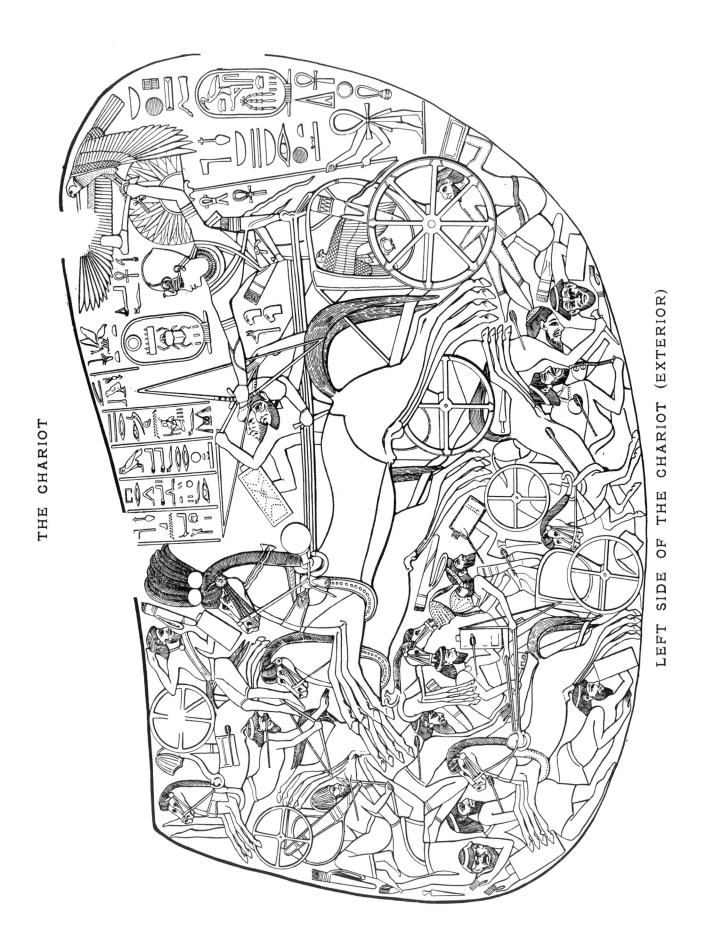

THE CHARIOT

LEFT SIDE OF THE CHARIOT (EXTERIOR)

the act of overthrowing consists of two distinct races of Asiatics, with pronounced
Semitic features (for details and types, see fig. 4, and compare with the list
given on the inside of the chariot). One of the tribes is characterised by long hair,
pointed beard, and small moustachios; the hair is bound round the crown by a
fillet; the features are large, the lips are thick, and there are signs of scoring on
the cheeks; their garments were of richly-decorated tapestry-woven stuffs, and
consisted of tight-fitting vests, either with or without sleeves, and short kilts
fastened by leathern belts. The second tribe is characterised by shaven heads, long
pointed beards, and small moustachios. The features are rather more refined than
those of the first group, but are, nevertheless, strongly Semitic in type. Their

Fig. 5.

garments were also of richly-decorated tapestry-woven stuffs, and consisted of long-
sleeved vests and long skirts reaching almost to the ankles, and fastened above by
leathern belts. A distinctive feature of this tribe appears to have been their
ornamented helmets, with long tassel (for specimen, see fig. 4). In several
cases circular amulets are worn round the neck by representatives of both tribes
(for specimen, see fig. 5). The armoury of these foreigners apparently consisted
of axes, daggers, and bows and arrows, with quivers, for offence, and rectangular
shields for defence.

Near-side panel (see Plate XI). This scene is similar to that of the off-side panel, but
the principal figures face the reverse way. The enemy that Thoutmôsis IV is

PLATE XII.

THE CHARIOT

LEFT SIDE OF THE CHARIOT (INTERIOR)

INSIDE. *Left-hand panel* (see Plate XII). Thoutmôsis IV, as a human-headed lion, tramples down his enemies. He is attired with closed hawk's wings, the royal wig with twisted tail, and ram's horns, and the *atef*-crown with two pendent uræi on either side; to the chin is attached a false beard. In front of him are his names

FIG. 7.

and titles. Over his back is a fan composed of feathers, and above it is a beetle with outspread wings, holding a ⊙–sign in its forelegs and a Ꝺ–ring in its hind legs. Underneath his paws are three overthrown Asiatic foes, representing three distinct races (for details see fig. 7). The inscription explanatory of this scene reads: [hieroglyphs]. Behind the king is standing a figure of the hawk-headed god Mentu, with arms and wings outspread. Upon his head the god wears a wig of medium length, and upon the top of it are two ostrich feathers and the sun's disc, with pendent double uræi. Around his neck he wears a necklace, and a coat of mail covers the body from breast to knees. In his right hand he holds the *khepsh*-sword, and three signs, [hieroglyphs], symbolising power, stability, and life. Above and behind the god is the following inscription in five vertical lines: (1) [hieroglyphs] (2) [hieroglyphs] (3) [hieroglyphs] (4) [hieroglyphs] (5) [hieroglyphs].

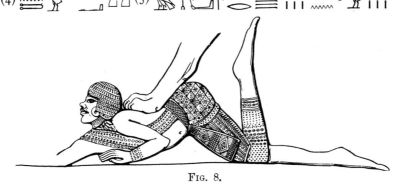

FIG. 8.

Right-hand panel. This scene is similar to that on the left-hand panel, except that the king faces ←, and is represented trampling on three of his Southern foes (for specimen, see fig. 8). The inscriptions, of course, also differ, and read as follows :—(*a*) Beneath the legs of the king : [hieroglyphs] . (*b*) Above the

god Mentu : (1) [hieroglyphs] (2) [hieroglyphs] (3) [hieroglyphs]

(4) [hieroglyphs]

Beneath both panels are lists of the conquered tribes: on the left side the Northerners, bound with papyrus flowers, and on the right side the Southerners, bound with lotus flowers.   The following is a list of them, together with their facial types :—

Left-hand side :

(1) [hieroglyphs] Naharaina.   See fig. 9.

(2) [hieroglyphs] Sangara.   See fig 10.

(3) [hieroglyphs] Tounipa.   See fig. 11.

(4) [hieroglyphs] Shasu.   See fig. 12.

(5) [hieroglyphs] Kadshi.   See fig. 13.

(6) [hieroglyphs] Tikhisa.   See fig. 14.

FIG. 9.

FIG. 10.

FIG. 11.

FIG. 12.

FIG. 13.

FIG. 14.

Right hand side :

(1)  . . . . . aa.   See fig. 15.

(2) Kalai.   See fig. 16.

(3) Mieóu.   See fig. 17.

(4) Ilima.   See fig. 18.

(5) Gourases.   See fig. 19.

(6) Diouraik.   See fig. 20.

FIG. 15.

FIG. 16.

FIG. 17.

FIG. 18.

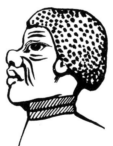

FIG. 19.

FIG. 20.

Beneath these again is another row of prisoners without names; they are bound by cords to ⟂-signs in either corner.

8. PARTS OF CHARIOT, LEATHER-WORK, ETC.

46098.   Saddle [1].—Wood, covered with red leather.—Height 0 m ·19.—
Span 0 m ·20.—Chamber 3.—See fig. 21.

Saddle, for yoking horse to chariot-pole.

FIG. 21.

46099.   Fragment of Saddle [2].—Wood, covered with red leather.—
Chamber 3.

Small fragment of saddle, similar to No. 1.

46100.   End of Pole [3].—Wood, covered with red leather.—Maximum
thickness 0 m ·04.—Maximum width 0 m ·06.—Chamber 4.—
See fig. 22.

Butt-end of chariot-pole, showing the dowelling to fit into socket.

FIG. 22.

46101.   Boss [4].—Leather and stucco.—Diameter 0 m ·054.—Chamber 3.

Circular green leather boss, with centre covered with stucco.

46102.   Rosette [5].—Bronze.—Diameter 0 m ·03.—Chamber 3.

Circular bronze rosette, probably from the trappings of the horses.

46103.   Pouch Flap [6].—Leather.—Length 0 m ·17.—Breadth 0 m ·22.—
Chamber 3.

Pouch flap, of leather, embossed with the following design: On the right and left side
are the nomen and prenomen of Thoutmôsis IV; in the centre is a hawk with
outstretched wings and sun's disc on head, clawing the head of a crouching figure
of a Northerner on the one side and a Southerner on the other. The inscription
□□ × ⌒⌒ ▽ describes the scene.
⌒⌒ ᗡ ⌒ ‖‖ ᗡ

[A number of other fragments of the chariot were found, but none of them could be
identified.]

46104.   Trapping [7].—Leather.—Length 0 m ·165.—Width 0 m ·085.—
Chamber 3.—Fig. 23.

Leather trapping, embossed with conventional floral design. There are remains of
stitching round the margin.

FIG. 23.   FIG. 24.

46105.   Trapping [8].   Leather.—Width 0 m ·11.—Chamber 3.—Fig. 24.

Leather trapping, embossed with a design showing Thoutmôsis IV as a sphinx
treading on a Syrian: above it is the cartouche (⊙ 🪲) and the words □□ ⌒⌒.
There are remains of stitching round the margin.

46106. **Boss** [9].—Leather.—Diameter 0 m ·083.—Chamber 3.—Fig. 25.

Leather boss, embossed with conventional floral design. There are remains of stitches round the margin.

Fig. 25.

Fig. 26.

46107. **Trapping** [10].—Leather.—Length 0 m ·14.—Wide 0 m ·048.— Chamber 3.—Fig. 26.

Embossed leather trapping, stained red, with green and red leather strips appliqued on to the margin. In the centre is the cartouche of Thoutmôsis IV surmounted by the ram's horns, sun's disc, and double feathers. Beneath, are two kneeling foreigners back to back and with arms upraised; underneath them is a ▽–sign.

46108. **Trapping** [11].—Leather.—Length 0 m ·24.—Breadth 0 m ·14.— Chamber 3.—Fig. 27.

Trapping, in leather applique.

Fig. 27.

Fig. 28.

46109. **Trapping** [12].—Leather.—Length 0 m ·13.—Breadth 0 m ·085.— Chamber 3.—Fig. 28.

Trapping, in leather applique.

46110. Trapping [13]. Leather.—Length 0 m ·21.—Breadth 0 m ·15.—Chamber [3].—Fig. 29.

Trapping, in leather applique.

FIG. 29.   FIG. 30

46111. Trapping [14].—Leather.—Length 0 m ·21.—Breadth 0 m ·11—Chamber 3.—Fig. 30.

FIG. 31.

46112. Gauntlet [15].—Leather.—Length 0 m ·32.—Chamber 3.—Fig. 31.

Gauntlet of the king, in red leather with green strips of leather sewn on the edges. The gauntlet is made to fit tightly on the wrist and loosely over the fore-arm; and with a guard for the thumb.

46113.   Fragments of a Gauntlet [16].—Leather.—Chamber 3.

Five fragments of a similar gauntlet to No. 46112.

46114.   Upper part Scabbard [17] —Leather.—Breadth 0 m ·05.—Room A.
—Fig. 32.

Upper part of scabbard for dagger in tooled leatherwork, having two strips of leather
at the back for attachment to a belt or leather strap.

FIG. 32.

46115.   Scabbard [18].—Leather.—Length   0   m   ·245.—Maximum   width
0 m ·03.—Chamber 3.—Fig. 33.

FIG. 33.

46116.   Fragments of Whip [19].—Leather.—Chamber 3.

Five fragments of the end of a whip and lash of red leather.   The stick was inlaid
with coloured barks.

46117.   Armlet [20].—Leather.—Breadth 0 m ·12.—Chamber 3.

Armlet in red leather.

46118.   Armlet [21].—Leather.—Breadth 0 m ·15.—Chamber 3.

Armlet in red leather.

[Thirty-one miscellaneous pieces of harness, trappings, sandals, leather bindings, etc.]

9. MISCELLANEOUS OBJECTS.

46119. **Fragment of a Draught-board** [1].—Wood, with glass inlay.—Length 0 m ·13.—Height 0 m ·055.—Width 0 m ·09.—Chamber 4.

Fragment of a wooden draught-board, inlaid above and below with squares composed of violet glass rods, divided by rods of yellow, blue, and yellow glass. The sides and ends are inlaid with violet glass rods arranged horizontally.

46120. **Fan-handle**(?) [2].—Wood, with ivory inlay.—Length 0 m ·10.—Chamber 4.

Fragment of a fan-handle (?) in wood, with ivory inlay. Along the margin is a band of coloured rectangles, and inside, a series of zigzags in ivory inlay, coloured respectively black, white, black, white, and red.

TECHNIQUE: very fine.

46121. **Fragment of Carved Wood** [3]. Cedar.—Length 9 m ·12.—Depth 0 m ·01.—Width 0 m ·019.—Chamber 4.

Fragment of wood carved in relief, with a continuous coil pattern above and a row of rectangles below. The under side is broken, and bears traces of white plaster.

46122. **Fragment of Carved Wood** [4].—Cedar.—Length 0 m ·12.—Depth 0 m ·01.—Width 0 m ·019.—Chamber 4.

Fragment of wood similar to No. 46121.

46123. **Label** [5].—Wood (pine).—Length 0 m ·099.—Width 0 m ·045.—Thickness 0 m ·007.—Room D.—Fig. 34.

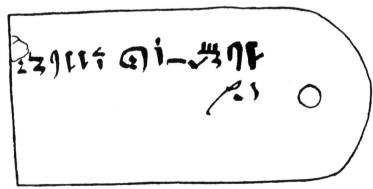

FIG. 34.

Wooden label, with hole for suspension, and bearing a hieratic inscription written in black ink.

46124. **Label** [6].—Wood (pine).—Length 0 m ·083.—Width 0 m ·034.—
Thickness 0 m ·007.—Chamber 4.—Fig. 35.

Wooden label, with hole for suspension, and bearing a hieratic inscription written in
black ink.

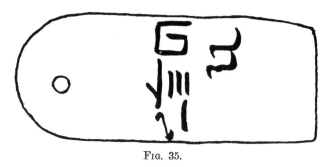

FIG. 35.

46125. **Label** [7].—Wood (pine).—Length 0 m ·085.—Width 0 m ·042.—
Thickness 0 m ·007.—Chamber 4.—Fig. 36.

Wooden label, with hole for suspension, and bearing a hieratic inscription written
upon it in black ink.

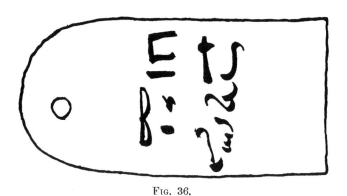

FIG. 36.

46126. **Label** [8].—Wood (pine).—Length 0 m ·083.—Width 0 m ·035.—
Thickness 0 m ·013.—Chamber 4.—Fig. 37.

FIG. 37.

Wooden label, with hole for suspension, and bearing a hieratic inscription written
upon it in black ink.

46127. Fragment of Box [9].—Wood (pine).—Length 0 m ·09.—Chamber 4.

Fragment of a wooden box, with the cartouche of Thoutmôsis IV incised upon it:

46128. End of the handle of a Battle-axe [10]. Wood (ebony).—Width 0 m ·065.—Breadth 0 m ·043.—Found in débris outside tomb.

End of the wooden handle of a battle-axe, inscribed with the cartouche of Thoutmôsis IV. The hieroglyphs are incised and filled in with white paint, and read:

. The section of the end is oval-shaped, and a mortice hole has been cut in it for fixing the handle.

46129. Pedestal for the foot of a Chair [11].—Wood, covered with canvas and stucco.—Height 0 m ·05.—Width of top 0 m ·075.—Width of base 0 m ·115.—Chamber 4.

Pedestal for the foot of a chair, in wood, covered with canvas and stucco. On the stucco on three sides are modelled designs showing a -sign, to which are bound two prisoners, representing the Northerners on the left and the Southerners on the right; on the fourth side is a mortice hole. The stucco appears to have been pinned round the edges with metal pins.

46130. Pedestal for the foot of a Chair [12].—Wood, painted.—Height 0 m ·08.—Width of top 0 m ·075.—Width of base 0 m ·105.—Chamber 4.

Pedestal for the foot of a chair, in wood, painted white, with a thick black line around the edges. On one side is a mortice hole.

46131. Pedestal for the foot of a Chair [13].—Wood, painted.—Height 0 m ·072.—Width of top 0 m ·065.—Width of base 0 m ·09.—Chamber 4.

Pedestal for the foot of a chair, similar to No. 12.

46132. Two fragments of a Shawabti Figure [14].—Wood, polished.—Chamber A.

Fragments of the face and foot of a shawabti figure, exquisitely carved.

46133. Fragments of Inlayed Wood [15].—Wood inlayed with glass.— Chamber 4.

Four fragments of wood, inlaid with glass. On one piece is the cartouche of Thoutmôsis IV : ⌇ ⌇ (⊙ ▨▨). The design on the remaining three pieces is the usual conventional feather pattern, executed in white and light blue glass, inlaid in plaster on the wood.

46134. Uas [16].—Wood.—Length 0 m ·145.—Found in débris outside tomb.

⌇, carved in wood, with tongues above and below for inserting into mortice holes.

46135. Fragments of a Box [17].—Wood, walnut.—Length 0 m ·42.— Depth 0 m ·35.—Chamber 3.

Fragments of the sides and ends of a plain walnut wood box.

46136. Four pieces of a Spoon [18].—Wood, cedar.—Chamber 3.

Four fragments of a plain wooden spoon, with long handle.

46137-46139. Three Pegs [19-21].—Wood.—Chamber 4.

Three wooden button-shaped pegs for boxes.

46140. Head of Walking Staff [22]. Wood.—Length 0 m ·12.—Diameter 0 m ·042.—Chamber 4.

Head of walking staff, in polished wood, with button-shaped top, and tongue for fixing into staff.

46141. Chair-legs [23].—Wood.—Chamber 4.

Two broken chair legs, with mortice hole at top; rough work.

46142. Bolt [24].—Wood, cedar.—Length 0 m ·145.—Width 0 m ·017.— Chamber 4.

Carved wooden —*— –shaped bolt.

46143. Spud [25].—Wood.—Length 0 m ·17.—Chamber 4.

Plasterer's spud.

46144. **Spud** [26].—Wood.—Length 0 m ·165.—Chamber 4.

Plasterer's spud.

46145. **Plumb-level** [27].—Wood.—Length 0 m ·16.—Diameter 0 m ·005.—Chamber 4.

Mason's plumb level, in wood of cylindrical form.

46146. **Plumb-level** [28].—Wood.—Length 0 m ·16.—Diameter 0 m ·005.—Chamber 4.

Similar to No. 46145. Broken at one end.

46147. **Three Supports** [29].—Wood.—Chamber 4.

Three wooden supports, covered with stucco, with wooden pins, and holes in the pins for metal tops (?).

46148. **Seven Supports** [30].—Wood.—Chamber 4.

Seven supports, in pine wood veneered with ebony. These are smaller than No. 46147.

46149. **Seven Supports** [31].—Wood.—Chamber 4.

Seven supports, similar to No. 46147, but grooved across.

46150. **Supports** [32].—Wood.—Chamber 4.

Pieces of similar supports to No. 46149, but larger, and coated with stucco.

46151. **Supports** [33].—Bone (?).—Chamber 4.

Supports, of bone (?), coated with green leather; one with traces of stucco.

46152. **Binding of a Vessel** [34].—String and clay.—Chamber 4.

Binding of a vessel, in string and cloth, sealed with a cartouche of Thoutmôsis .

46153. **Weight** [35].—Flint.—Chamber 1.

Natural flint weight, with written upon it in black ink.

6.

46154.   Fragment of Mirror-Handle [36].—Ivory.—Maximum length 0 m ·08. —Minimum length 0 m ·035.—Chamber 8.

Fragment of a papyrus-shaped ivory handle to a mirror.

46155.   Fragments of Mace-heads [37].—Crystalline limestone.—Chamber 4.

Fragments of two small crystalline limestone mace-heads (broken); one with flutings.

46156.   Fragment of (?) [38].—Crystalline limestone.—Chamber 4.

Fragment of crystalline limestone, of cylindrical form, bearing the cartouche of Thoutmôsis IV.

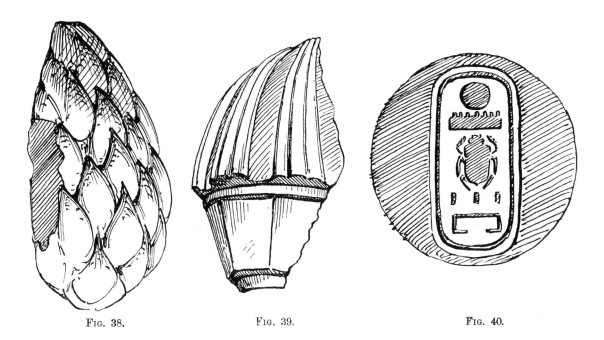

FIG. 38.   FIG. 39.   FIG. 40.

46157.   Fragment of Mace-head [39].—Wood.—Chamber 3.—See fig. 38.

Fragment of a mace-head, modelled in the form of a pine cone, and similar to one represented in the hand of Sety I in the Osiris chapel at Abydos.

46158.   Fragment of Mace-head [40].—Clouded agate.—Chamber D.— See fig. 39.

Fragment of a clouded agate mace-head.

46159.   Sealings [41].—Mud.—Chamber C.—See fig. 40.

Several mud sealings of jars, with cartouche of Thoutmôsis IV.

PLATE XIII.

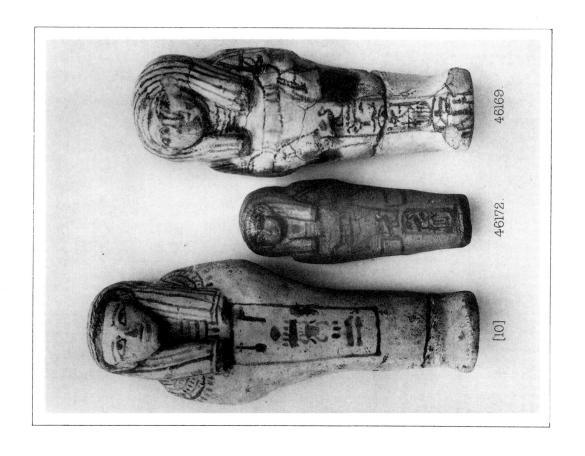

SHAWABTI FIGURES.

10. SHAWABTI FIGURES.

46160. **Lower part of a Shawabti figure** [1].—White and violet glazed faïence.—Length 0 m ·083.—Breadth 0 m ·045.—Chamber 3.— Plate XIII.

Lower part of a shawabti figure, in the form of a mummy, of white glazed faïence, with hieroglyphs, dividing lines, and other ornamentation in dark violet glaze. Around the front of the figure are eight horizontal lines of hieroglyphs, and down the back two vertical lines, giving the following part of the Sixth Chapter of the Book of the Dead:

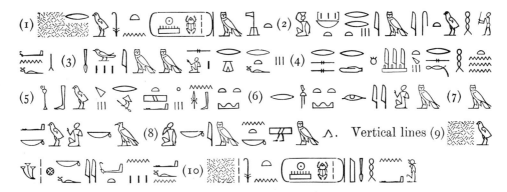

Upon the soles of the feet is a figure of Isis standing upon a ⌐⌐⌐-sign. She has her arms upraised, and on either side of her are the following hieroglyphs:

The quality of the glaze is very fine, and the colour is perfect, without a flaw or blemish.

TECHNIQUE: very fine.

46161. **Shawabti Figure** [2].—Blue glazed faïence.—Length 0 m ·185.— Breadth 0 m ·055.—Room D.—Plate XIII.

Shawabti figure, in the form of a royal mummy. The head-dress represents a linen cloth stretched tightly across the forehead, folded behind the ears, and falling down over the front of the shoulders to the chest; upon it, in the centre of the forehead, is affixed a uræus serpent, and from behind, at the nape of the neck, issues a small twisted pigtail. On the chin is a "false" beard. The eyes, eyebrows, and other features of the face are modelled and emphasized by black lines. The arms are folded over the chest, and the body is shown swathed in a winding-sheet, from which the hands protrude. Down the front of the figure is a vertical column of hieroglyphs painted in black, giving the name and titles of Thoutmôsis IV, and reading:

The quality of the glazing and technique is very fine; the colouring is remarkable for its purity.

Broken into two pieces.

—   **Shawabti Figure** [3].—Blue glazed faïence—Length 0 m ·185.— Breadth 0 m ·055.—Room D.—Plate XIII.

Shawabti figure in the form of a royal mummy. Modelling, ornamentation, and inscription same as No. 46161.

The quality of the glazing and technique is fine; the colouring remarkable for its purity.

Broken into two pieces.

[Davis Collection.]

—   **Shawabti Figure** [4].—Blue glazed faïence.—Length 0 m ·185.— Breadth 0 m ·055.—Room D.

Shawabti figure, in the form of a royal mummy. Modelling, ornamentation, and inscription same as No. 46161.

The quality of the glazing and technique is fine; the colouring remarkable for its purity.

Broken into four pieces.

[Davis Collection.]

46162.   **Shawabti Figure** [5].—Blue glazed faïence.—Length 0 m ·185 (?).— Breadth 0 m ·055.—Room D.

Shawabti figure, in the form of a royal mummy. Modelling, ornamentation, and inscription same as No. 46161.

The quality of the glazing and technique is good; colouring, a deep blue.

Broken; three pieces (piece wanting from centre of figure).

46163.   **Shawabti Figure** [6].—Blue glazed faïence.—Length 0 m ·185 (?).— Breadth 0 m ·055 (?).—Room D.

Shawabti figure, in the form of a royal mummy. Modelling, ornamentation, and inscription same as No. 46161.

The quality of the glazing and technique is good; colouring, a medium blue.

Broken; two pieces (piece wanting from centre of figure).

46164. **Shawabti Figure** [7].—Blue glazed faïence.—Length 0 m ·185 (?).—
Breadth 0 m ·055 (?).—Room D.

Shawabti figure, in the form of a royal mummy. Modelling, ornamentation, and
inscription same as No. 46161.

The quality of the glazing and technique, poor; colouring, a medium blue.

Broken; two pieces (pieces wanting from centre of figure).

46165. **Lower part of a Shawabti Figure** [8].—Blue glazed faïence.—
Room D.

Lower part of a shawabti figure, in the form of a royal mummy.

Quality of glazing and technique, good; colour, a deep blue.

Broken; one piece (the whole of the upper part of the figure wanting).

46166. **Lower part of a Shawabti Figure** [9].—Blue glazed faïence.—
Room D.

Lower part of a shawabti figure, in the form of a royal mummy.

Quality of glazing and technique, good; colour, a deep blue.

Broken; one piece (the whole of the upper part of the figure wanting).

— **Shawabti Figure** [10].—Blue glazed faïence.—Length 0 m ·020.—
Breadth 0 m ·075.—Room D.—Plate XIII, [10].

Shawabti figure, in the form of a mummy. The wig is long, falls down in front over
the shoulders, and the hair is represented by black parallel lines. The features
of the face are modelled, and emphasized by black lines. Around the neck
and shoulders is shown a deep necklace with rows of bugle-shaped pendants.
The arms are crossed over the chest, but the hands do not protrude from
the winding-sheet which covers the body. Down the front of the figure is a
vertical column of hieroglyphs giving the name and titles of Thoutmôsis IV:

Quality of glaze and technique, fair; colour, medium blue.

Broken into two pieces.

[Davis Collection.]

46167. **Shawabti Figure** [11].—Blue glazed faïence.—Length 0 m ·22.—
Breadth 0 m ·08.—Room D.

Shawabti figure, in the form of a mummy. Modelling, ornamentation, and inscription
same as No. [10].

Quality of glaze and technique, medium; colour, medium blue.

Broken into two pieces.

46168.   Shawabti Figure [12].—Blue glazed faïence.—Length 0 m ·235.– Breadth 0 m ·07.—Room D.

Modelling, ornamentation, and inscription same as No. [10].

Quality of glaze and technique, medium ; colour, medium blue.

Broken into three pieces.

46169.   Shawabti Figure [13].—Blue glazed faïence.—Length 0 m ·18.— Breadth 0 m ·07.—Room D.—Plate XIII.

Shawabti figure, in the form of a mummy.   The wig is long, falls down in front over the shoulders, and the hair is represented by parallel lines painted in black.   The features of the face are only roughly modelled, but they are emphasized by black lines.   Around the neck and shoulders is shown a broad necklace of parallel strings of beads.   The arms are crossed over the chest, and the hands are represented protruding from the winding-sheet, holding hoes, outlined in black, while at the back of the figure is depicted the workman's basket.   Down the front of the figure is a vertical line of hieroglyphs painted in black, giving the name of Thoutmôsis IV :

Quality of glaze and technique, poor and rough ; colour, medium blue.

Broken into two pieces.

Shawabti Figure [14].—Blue glazed faïence.—Length 0 m ·19.— Breadth 0 m ·07.—Room D.

Shawabti figure, in the form of a mummy.   Modelling and ornamentation similar to No. 46169, except that on the soles of the feet of this specimen is drawn in black a papyrus plant with leaves thus :   .   The inscription is also the same as that on No. [13], except that after the word *mery* is written   .

Quality of glaze and technique, fine ; colour, a medium blue.

Broken into two pieces.

[Davis Collection.]

46170.   Shawabti Figure [15].—Blue glazed faïence.—Length 0 m ·185.— Breadth 0 m ·07.—Room D.

Shawabti figure in the form of a mummy.   Modelling and ornamentation similar to No. 46169.   Down the front of the figure is a vertical line of hieroglyphs, painted in black, reading :   .

Quality of glaze and technique, fine ; colour, medium blue.

Broken into two pieces.

46171.   Shawabti Figure [16].—Blue glazed faïence.—Room D.

Shawabti figure in the form of a mummy. The inscription gives the prenomen of Thoutmôsis IV :

Quality of glaze and technique, fine ; colour, medium blue.

Broken ; one piece (the whole of the upper part of the figure wanting).

46172.   Shawabti Figure [17].—Blue glazed faïence.—Length 0 m ·125.— Breadth 0 m ·045.—Room D.—Plate XIII.

Shawabti figure in the form of a mummy. The wig is long, and falls down over the front to the shoulders. The features are emphasized by black lines. Around the neck and shoulders is shown a broad necklace of parallel strings of beads painted in black. The arms are crossed over the chest, and the hands are represented holding hoes and workmen's baskets ; the latter, shown suspended over the shoulders by a cord, fall down behind the figure. Down the front of the figure is a vertical line of hieroglyphs, giving the nomen of Thoutmôsis IV :

Quality of glaze and technique, very good ; colour, a fine blue.

Unbroken.

—   Shawabti Figure [18].—Blue glazed faïence.—Length 0 m ·135.— Breadth 0 m ·045.—Room D.

Shawabti figure in the form of a mummy. Modelling and ornamentation similar to No. 46172. The inscription gives the prenomen of Thoutmôsis IV :

QUALITY OF GLAZE, good ; colour, a fine blue.

Broken into two pieces.

[Davis Collection.]

46173.   Shawabti Figure [19].—Blue glazed faïence.—Length 0 m ·135.— Breadth 0 m ·045.—Room D.

Shawabti figure in the form of a mummy. Modelling and ornamentation similar to No. 46172. The inscription gives the prenomen of Thoutmôsis IV :

QUALITY OF GLAZE, medium ; colour, medium blue.

Broken into two pieces.

46174.   Shawabti Figure [20].—Blue glazed faïence.—Length 0 m ·135.—
Breadth 0 m ·05.—Room D.

Shawabti figure in the form of a mummy.   Modelling and ornamentation similar
to No. 46172.   The inscription gives the prenomen of Thoutmôsis IV :

QUALITY OF GLAZE, medium; colour, medium blue.

Broken into two pieces.

46175.   Shawabti Figure [21].—Blue glazed faïence.—Length 0 m ·075.—
Breadth 0 m ·035.—Room D.

Shawabti figure in the form of a mummy, with wig.   Uninscribed.

QUALITY OF GLAZE, poor; colour, medium blue; in a bad state of preservation.

Broken into two pieces.

46176.   Shawabti Figure [22].—Blue glazed faïence.—Length 0 m ·075 (?).—
Breadth 0 m ·03.—Room D.

Shawabti figure in the form of a mummy.   Similar to No. 46175.   Uninscribed.

QUALITY OF GLAZE, medium; colour, medium blue.

Broken off below the ankles; feet wanting.

 —   **Shawabti Figure** [23].—Blue glazed faïence.—Length 0 m ·075 (?).—
Breadth 0 m ·025.—Room D.

Shawabti figure in the form of a mummy.   Similar to No. 46175.   Uninscribed.

QUALITY OF GLAZE, medium; colour, medium blue.

Broken off below the ankles; feet wanting.

[Davis Collection.]

 —   **Shawabti Figure** [24].—Dark violet glazed faïence.—Length 0 m ·075.
—Breadth 0 m ·025.—Room D.

Shawabti figure in the form of a mummy.   Similar to No. 46175.   Uninscribed.

QUALITY OF GLAZE, good; colour, rich dark violet.

Broken into two pieces.

[Davis Collection.]

— **Shawabti Figure** [25].—Dark violet glazed faïence.—Length (?).—Breadth 0 m ·027.—Room D.

Shawabti figure in the form of a mummy. Similar to No. 46175. Uninscribed.

QUALITY OF GLAZE, good ; colour, rich dark violet.

Broken off below the ankles ; feet missing.

[Davis Collection.]

— **Shawabti Figure** [26].—Dark violet glazed faïence.—Length (?).—Breadth 0 m ·025.—Room D.

Shawabti figure in the form of a mummy. Similar to No. 46175. Uninscribed.

QUALITY OF GLAZE, good ; colour, rich dark violet.

Broken off below the ankles ; feet missing.

[Davis Collection.]

46177. **Shawabti Figure** [27].—Blue glazed faïence.—Length 0 m ·12.—Breadth 0 m ·025.—Room D.

Shawabti figure in the form of a mummy, wearing wig (lined black), and with features of face modelled. Uninscribed.

QUALITY OF GLAZE, medium ; colour, medium blue.

Broken into two pieces.

46178. **Shawabti Figure** [28].—Blue glazed faïence.—Length 0 m ·13.—Breadth 0 m ·025.—Room D.

Shawabti figure in form of a mummy, wearing wig (lined black), and with features of face modelled and emphasized with black lines. Inscribed on breast : .

QUALITY OF GLAZE, medium ; colour, medium blue.

Broken into two pieces.

46179. **Shawabti Figure** [29].—Blue glazed faïence.—Length ?.—Breadth 0 m ·025.—Room D.

Shawabti figure, in the form of a mummy, wearing wig and necklace. Inscribed on chest as No. 46178.

QUALITY OF GLAZE, medium ; colour, medium blue.

Broken, feet wanting.

46180.　Shawabti Figure [30].—Blue glazed faïence.—Length 0 m ·105.—
　　　　Breadth 0 m ·03.—Room D.

Shawabti figure, in the form of a mummy, as No. 46179.　Inscription on chest as
No. 46178.

QUALITY OF GLAZE, medium; colour, medium blue.

Complete.

PLATE XIV.

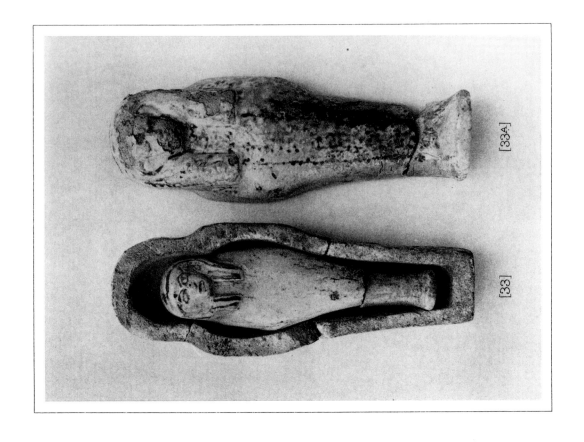

[33A] [33]

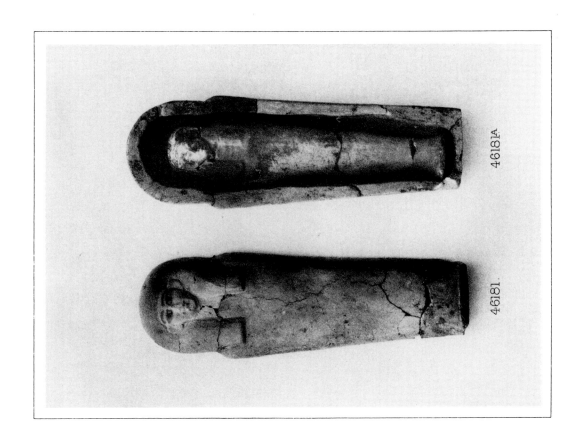

46181A 46181.

MODEL COFFINS & FIGURES.

11. MODEL COFFINS WITH SHAWABTI FIGURES.

46181. **Model Coffin with Shawabti Figure** [31].—Blue glazed faïence.—Room D.—Plate XIV.

MODEL COFFIN: *Lid*, shaped to represent the upper half of a mummy, with wig and features of face modelled. Length 0 m ·18.—Breadth 0 m ·057.

Broken into four pieces.

Box, shaped to represent the lower half of a mummy. Length 0 m ·18.—Breadth 0 m ·057.—Depth 0 m ·03.

Broken into six pieces.

SHAWABTI FIGURE, in the form of a mummy, wearing wig and necklace; features of face modelled. Length 0 m ·15.—Breadth 0 m ·035.

Broken into five pieces.

QUALITY OF GLAZE, good; colour, a fine deep blue.

46182. **Model Coffin with Shawabti Figure** [32].—Blue glazed faïence.—Room D.

MODEL COFFIN: *Lid*, similar to No. 46181. Length 0 m ·175.—Breadth 0 m ·055.
Broken into two pieces.

Box, similar to No. 46181. Length 0 m ·175.—Breadth 0 m ·055.—Depth 0 m ·03.

Broken, seven pieces; incomplete.

SHAWABTI FIGURE, in the form of a mummy, similar to No. 46181.—Breadth 0 m ·032.

Broken into two pieces; incomplete.

QUALITY OF GLAZE, good; colour, a fine deep blue.

Model Coffin with Shawabti Figure [33].—Blue glazed faïence.—Room D.--Plate XIV, [33], [33A].

MODEL COFFIN: *Lid*, shaped to represent the upper half of a mummy, with wig and features of face modelled. Down the front of it is a vertical line of hieroglyphs reading ⸗. Length 0 m ·20.—Breadth 0 m ·07
Broken into two pieces.

Box, shaped to represent the lower half of a mummy. Same dimensions as lid, with depth of 0 m ·03.

Broken into three pieces.

SHAWABTI FIGURE, in the form of a mummy, with wig and face modelled, the wig ending in a twist behind. Length 0 m ·155.—Breadth 0 m ·045.

Broken into two pieces.

QUALITY OF GLAZE, good, but the model coffin is not glazed on the inside or on the edges, and it has flaked in parts on the lid. The colour is a fine blue.

[Davis Collection.]

46183. Model Coffin with Shawabti Figure [34].—Blue glazed faïence.— Room D.

MODEL COFFIN: *Lid*, similar to that of No. [33], but without the inscription. Length 0 m ·21.—Breadth 0 m ·75.

Broken into four pieces.

Box, similar to that of No. [33]. Same dimensions as lid, and with a depth of 0 m ·03.

Broken into four pieces.

SHAWABTI FIGURE, in the form of a mummy, as that of No. [33]. Length (?).— Breadth 0 m ·045.

Broken ; the feet wanting.

QUALITY OF GLAZE, rough, but the model coffin is not glazed on the inside. Colour, medium blue.

46184. Lid of a Model Coffin [35].—Blue glazed faïence.—Room D.

Shaped to represent the upper half of a mummy, with modelled face, and wearing wig and necklace, the latter outlined in black. On the breast is the nomen of the king written in black: Length 0 m ·195.—Breadth 0 m ·065.

Broken into four pieces.

46185. Lid of a Model Coffin [36].—Blue glazed faïence.—Room D.— Plate XV.

Shaped and inscribed as No. 46184. Length 0 m ·205.—Breadth 0 m ·065.

Broken into three pieces.

46186. Lid of a Model Coffin [37].—Blue glazed faïence.— Room D.

Shaped as No. 46184. Inscribed with prenomen of Thoutmôsis IV: Length 0 m ·20. Breadth 0 m ·075.

Broken into three pieces.

46187. Lid of a Model Coffin [38].—Blue glazed faïence.—Room D.

Shaped and inscribed as No. 46186. Length 0 m ·20.—Breadth 0 m ·065.

Broken into two pieces.

PLATE XV.

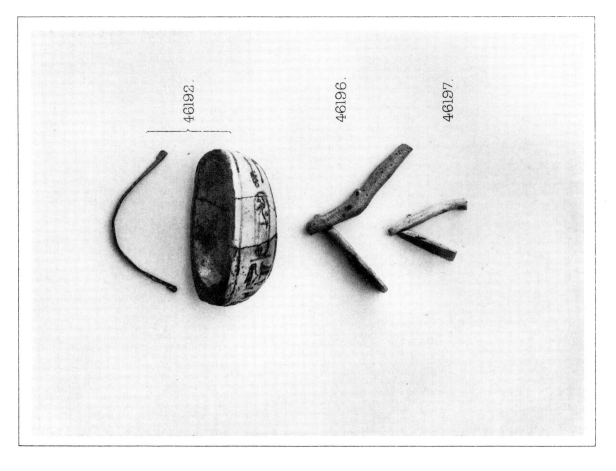

46192.

46196.

46197.

MODEL BASKET & HOES.

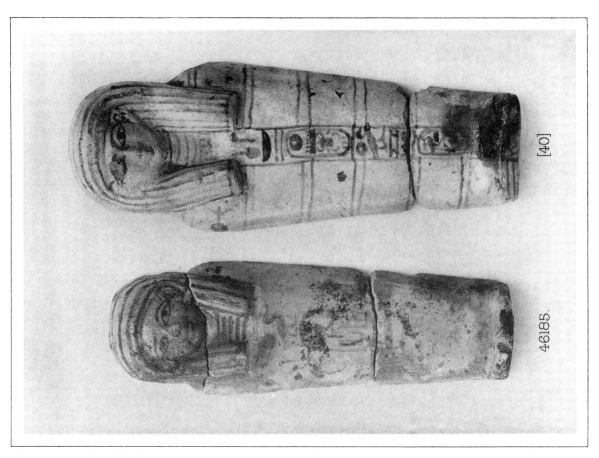

[40]

46185.

LIDS OF MODEL COFFINS.

46188. Model Coffin [39].—Blue glazed faïence.—Room D.

Lid and *box*, shaped to represent a mummy, with face modelled, and wearing wig. The body is shown as if bound with three linen bands, indicated by double vertical lines. Down the front of the figure is a vertical line of hieroglyphs written in black, reading: [hieroglyphs] , while on the foot of the lid is an eye [hieroglyph] and on the foot of the box a [hieroglyph]. On the rim of the box is an ornament composed of rectangles drawn in horizontal and vertical black lines.

QUALITY OF GLAZE, medium; colour, medium blue. (Glazed inside.)

Broken into nine pieces; incomplete.

— **Model Coffin** [40].—Blue glazed faïence.—Room D.—Plate XV [40].

Lid and *box* shaped to represent a mummy, with face modelled, and wearing wig. Down the front of the lid is an inscription written in black ink, reading: [hieroglyphs], while on one side is a [hieroglyph]-sign and on the bottom is a [hieroglyph]-sign. Length 0 m ·025.—Breadth 0 m ·085.

QUALITY OF GLAZE, good; colour, a fine medium blue on the outside, violet on the inside.

Broken into four pieces.

[Davis Collection.]

46189. Model Coffin [41].—Blue glazed faïence.—Room D.

Lid and *box* shaped as No. [40]. Inscription, [hieroglyphs] [hieroglyphs]; on the foot of lid, drawn in black, is a [hieroglyph]-chair. Length 0 m ·225.— Breadth 0 m ·09.—Depth 0 m ·035.

QUALITY OF GLAZE, medium; colour, medium blue.

Broken into four pieces; incomplete.

46190. Model Coffin [42].—Blue glazed faïence.—Room D and Chamber 4.

Lid and *box* shaped as No. [40]. Inscription, [hieroglyphs]. Length (?).—Breadth 0 m ·09.—Depth 0 m ·035.

QUALITY OF GLAZE, fair; colour, medium blue.

Broken into five pieces; incomplete.

46191. Model Coffin [43].—Blue glazed faïence.—Room D.

Similar lid to that of No. [40].

Broken, two fragments (only the head and feet remain).

12. MODEL BASKETS, HOES, ETC., FOR SHAWABTI FIGURES.

46192. **Model Basket** [44].—Blue glazed faïence.—Length 0 m ·075. Width 0 m ·05.—Depth 0 m ·035.—Room D.—Plate XV.

Model basket for a shawabti figure in blue glazed faïence, ornamented with lines and hieroglyphs in violet. Pierced at both ends for suspension.

ORNAMENTATION: rim of basket, and bottom, violet. Along one side runs an inscription, written lengthwise, reading:

QUALITY OF GLAZE, good; colour, medium blue.

Broken into five pieces; complete.

A thin bronze yoke, 0 m ·07 long, found in Room D, probably belonged to this basket.

46193. **Model Basket** [45].—Blue glazed faïence.—Length 0 m ·075. Width 0 m ·035.—Depth 0 m ·045.—Room D.

Model basket for a shawabti figure, in blue glazed faïence, and pierced at either end for suspension. On one side of it is written vertically the prenomen of Thoutmôsis IV in a cartouche:

QUALITY OF GLAZE, good; colour, medium blue.

Broken into five pieces (incomplete).

46194. **Model Basket** [46].—Blue glazed faïence.—Length 0 m ·07. Width 0 m ·03.—Depth 0 m ·04.—Room D.

Model basket for a shawabti figure in blue glazed faïence, and pierced for suspension. No ornamentation.

QUALITY OF GLAZE, good; colour, medium blue.

Broken into two pieces (a piece wanting from one side).

46195. **Model Basket** [47].—Blue glazed faïence.—Length 0 m ·07. Width 0 m ·03.—Depth 0 m ·04.—Chamber 3.

Model basket for a shawabti figure in blue glazed faïence, and pierced for suspension. Remains of thread in one hole.

QUALITY OF GLAZE, good; colour, medium blue.

Ten pieces, incomplete.

46196. **Model Hoe** [48].—Blue glazed faïence.—Length of blade 0 m ·05.—Width of blade 0 m ·02.—Chamber 3.—Plate XV.

Model hoe for a shawabti figure in blue glazed faïence. The blade is pierced with two holes for the insertion of string to tie it to the handle. The handle is broken at one end.

QUALITY OF GLAZE, good; colour, light blue.

46197. **Model Hoe** [49].—Blue glazed faïence.—Length of blade 0 m ·035.—Width of blade 0 m ·015.—Length of handle 0 m ·042.—Diameter of handle 0 m ·005.—Chamber 3.—Plate XV.

Model hoe for a shawabti figure, in blue glazed faïence, similar to No. 46196, but complete.

QUALITY OF GLAZE, good; colour, light blue.

46198. **Model Hoe** [50].—Blue glazed faïence.—Width of blade 0 m ·015.—Length of handle 0 m ·045.—Diameter of handle 0 m ·006.—Chamber 3.

Model hoe for a shawabti figure, in blue glazed faïence, similar to No. 46196, but complete.

QUALITY OF GLAZE, good; colour, light blue.

46199. **Model Hoe** [51].—Blue glazed faïence.—Length of blade 0 m ·025.—Width of blade 0 m ·015.—Diameter of handle 0 m ·008.—Chamber 3.

Model hoe for a shawabti figure, in blue glazed faïence, similar to No. 46196. The handle is broken at one end.

QUALITY OF GLAZE, good; colour, light blue.

46200-1. **Two Fragments of Model Hoes** [52-3].—Blue glazed faïence.—Chamber 3.

Two fragments of model hoes for a shawabti figure, in blue glazed faïence, similar to No. 46196.

46202. **Model Pick** [54].—Blue glazed faïence.—Length of blade 0 m ·05.—Width of blade 0 m ·007.—Length of handle 0 m ·075.—Diameter of handle 0 m ·008.

Model pick for a shawabti figure, in blue glazed faïence. The binding string is missing.

QUALITY OF GLAZE, good; colour, light blue.

Perfect.

13. CYLINDRICAL LIBATION VASES.

—— **Cylindrical Libation Vase** [1].—Blue glazed faïence.—Height 0 m ·12.—Maximum diameter 0 m ·16.—Room D.—Plate XVI. [1 and 1a.]

Cylindrical libation vase, in blue glazed faïence, ornamented with designs outlined in black.

ORNAMENTATION: *Spherical top*, around the mouth is (1) a narrow band of rectangles, (2) a band of plain blue, (3) a band of diamond-shaped lozenges, and (4) a row of nine lotus flowers with painted petals, each flower being separated from the next by three incurved and three recurved lines. Outside this band of lotus flowers is a narrow row of rectangles separating the ornamentation of the spherical top from that of the bowl.

Bowl. Around the circumference is (1) at the top, a broad band of diamond-shaped lozenges with black centres, (2) a band of scales in three rows, separated by (3) a narrow row of rectangles from (4) the band beneath, which consists of an alternating pattern of a papyrus flowers, a papyrus bud, and a lotus leaf. At the bottom is a row of rectangles. On the front of the vase is an inscription in three vertical columns, which interrupts the ornamentation, reading:—

QUALITY OF GLAZE, fine; colour, medium blue (stained in places).

Broken into eight pieces; almost complete.

Stopper.—Blue glazed faïence.—Height 0 m ·06.—Diameter 0 m ·07.

In the shape of an inverted lotus flower.

[Davis Collection.]

46203. Cylindrical Libation Vase [2].—Blue glazed faïence.—Height 0 m ·115.—Maximum diameter 0 m ·15.—Room D.—Plate XVII.

Cylindrical libation vase, in blue glazed faïence, ornamented with designs outlined in black.

PLATE XVI.

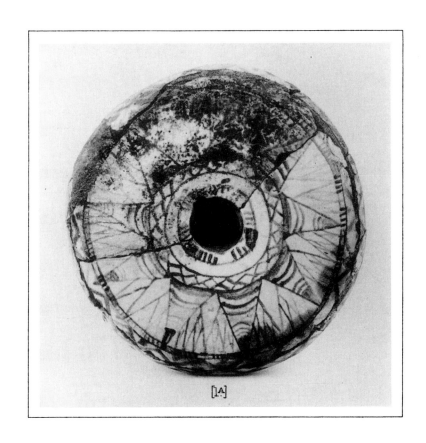

[1A]

[1]

LIBATION VASE

PLATE XVII.

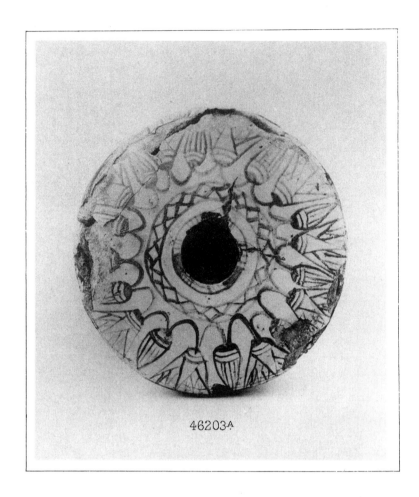

46203ᴬ

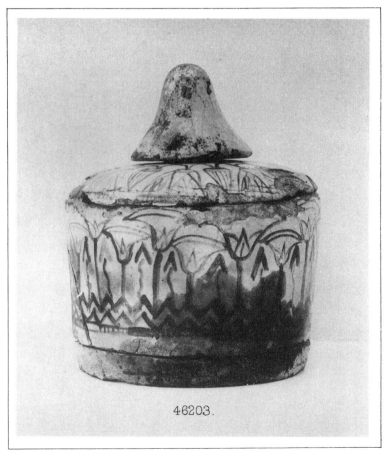

46203.

LIBATION VASE

ORNAMENTATION: *Spherical top*, around the mouth is (1) a narrow band of rectangles, (2) a band of plain blue, (3) a band of diamond-shaped lozenges, and (4) a row of lotus flowers with painted petals alternating with lotus buds. Outside this band of lotus flowers is a narrow row of rectangles, separating the ornamentation of the spherical top from that of the bowl.

Bowl, around the circumference is a row of papyrus flowers alternating with lotus leaves, and beneath it are two zigzag lines, representing the water from which the plants are supposed to spring.

QUALITY OF GLAZE, fine ; colour, medium blue.

Broken into several pieces ; part of one side missing.

Stopper.—Blue glazed faïence.—Height 0 m ·06.—Diameter 0 m ·07.

In the shape of an inverted lotus flower.

46204. Cylindrical Libation Vase [3].—Blue glazed faïence.—Height 0 m ·11.—Maximum diameter 0 m ·13.—Room D and Chamber 4.—Plate XVIII.

Cylindrical libation vase, in blue glazed faïence, ornamented with designs outlined in black.

ORNAMENTATION: *Spherical top*, around the mouth is a band of rounded black petals and a narrow black line.

Bowl, on the front of the vase is an inscription in three vertical columns, reading :

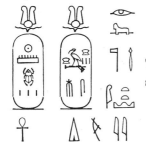

This inscription is enclosed in narrow black lines and surmounted by a broad ▭–sign.

Around the circumference of the vase is a design consisting of (1) Bennu birds with human arms and hands, seated on ▽–signs, alternating with (2) a group of hieroglyphs arranged thus :   . Within the loop of each ♀ is a   .

QUALITY OF GLAZE, very fine ; colour, a brilliant medium blue.

Broken into several pieces ; complete.

Stopper.—Blue glazed faïence.—Height 0 m ·06.—Diameter 0 m ·08.

In the form of an inverted lotus flower with rosette at the apex. Broken.

46205. Cylindrical Libation Vase [4].—Blue glazed faïence.—Height 0 m ·115.—Maximum diameter 0 m ·13.—Room D.—Plate XVIII.

Cylindrical libation vase, in blue glazed faïence, with designs outlined in black.

8.

ORNAMENTATION: *Spherical top,* immediately around the mouth are three black rings, and outside these a band of sharply-pointed lotus petals divided from the bowl by a black line.

Bowl, around the circumference is a scale pattern, which reaches from top to bottom of the bowl. On the front of it is an inscription in a rectangular panel, which interrupts the scale pattern ornamentation, and reads:

Around the circumference at the base is a narrow black line.

QUALITY OF GLAZE, very fine; colour, a very brilliant blue.

Broken into several pieces.

Stopper.—Blue glazed faïence.—Height 0 m ·055.—Diameter 0 m ·07.

In the shape of an inverted lotus flower, with rosette at the apex.

—   **Cylindrical Libation Vase** [5].—Blue glazed faïence.—Height 0 m ·10.—Maximum diameter 0 m ·13.—Chamber 3, near Chariot. —Plate XIX [5 and 5a].

Cylindrical libation vase, in blue glazed faïence, ornamented with designs outlined in black.

ORNAMENTATION: *Spherical top,* around the mouth is (1) a narrow band of rectangles, (2) a band of plain blue, (3) another band of rectangles, and (4) a row of lotus flowers with recurved sepals, alternating with lotus buds and lotus flowers with sharply-pointed petals. Outside this is a narrow band of rectangles dividing the spherical top from the bowl.

Bowl, around the circumference is painted a design representing a large ⚱-sign with upraised arms on either side of it; to the elbows of these arms are suspended ☥-signs. Alternating with this device are (1) the nomen and (2) the prenomen of Thoutmôsis IV in cartouches surmounted by ☉-signs. Around the circumference at the base is a broad band of black.

QUALITY OF GLAZE, very fine; colour, a brilliant blue.

Broken into several pieces.

Stopper.—Blue glazed faïence.—Height 0 m ·05.—Diameter 0 m ·05.

In the form of an inverted lotus flower with hair sepals.

[Davis Collection.]

PLATE XVIII.

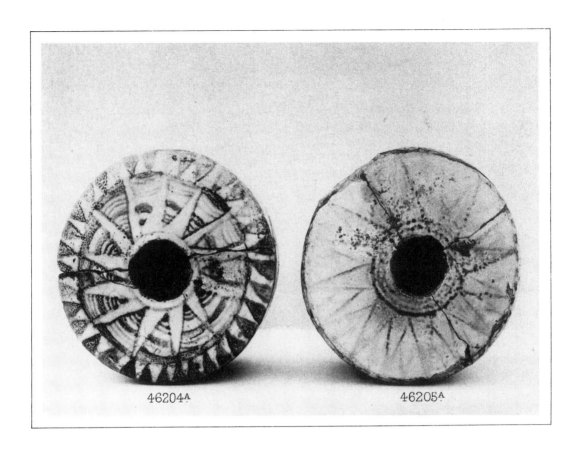

46204ᴬ   46205ᴬ

46204.   46205.

LIBATION VASES.

PLATE XIX.

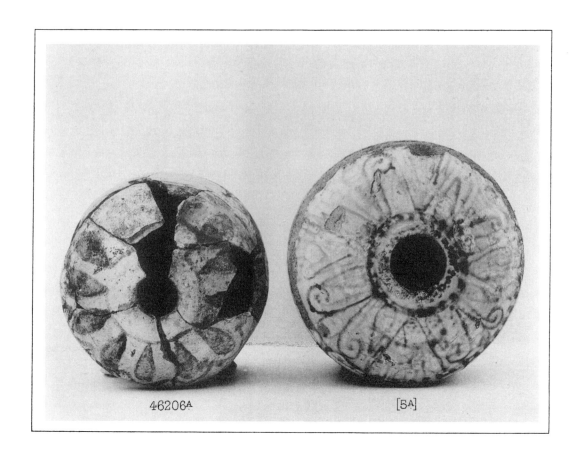

46206ᴬ   [5ᴬ]

46206.   [5]

LIBATION VASES.

46206. Cylindrical Libation Vase [6].—Blue glazed faïence.—Height 0 m ·115.—Diameter 0 m ·11.—Room D.—Plate XIX.

Cylindrical libation vase, in blue glazed faïence, ornamented with designs written in black.

ORNAMENTATION : *Spherical top,* around the mouth is a broad band of plain blue, outside which is a row of black drop-shaped petals, with a curved line following the outline of the lower part of the petals. Separating the spherical top from the bowl are two narrow black lines.

Bowl, around the circumference is a band of scales with black bases, arranged in three rows, and interrupted in the front by the prenomen of Thoutmôsis IV in a narrow rectangular panel. Around the circumference, at the base, is (1) a black line, (2) a narrow, plain blue band, and (3) a band of rectangles.

QUALITY OF GLAZE, medium ; colour, a dull blue.

Broken into several fragments, incomplete.

Stopper.—Blue glazed faïence.—Height 0 m ·05.—Diameter 0 m ·055.

In the shape of an inverted lotus flower, with hair sepals and black spot at apex.

46207. Cylindrical Libation Vase [7].—Blue glazed faïence.—Height 0 m ·12.—Maximum diameter 0 m ·125.—Room D.

Cylindrical libation vase, in blue glazed faïence, ornamented with designs written in black.

ORNAMENTATION : *Spherical top*; the mouth is broken away, but around it was (1) a row of wedge-shaped petals, painted in black; (2) two wavy lines, and (3) a black line separating the spherical top from the bowl.

Bowl, ornamentation similar to that of No. 46206.

QUALITY OF GLAZE, medium ; colour, a dull blue.

Broken into several pieces; parts of top and sides missing.

46208. Fragments of a Cylindrical Libation Vase [8].—Blue glazed faïence.—Height 0 m ·116.—Maximum diameter 0 m ·10.—Room D.

Fragments of a cylindrical libation vase, in blue glazed faïence, with ornamentation outlined in black.

ORNAMENTATION : *Spherical top,* similar to that of No. 46206.

Bowl, similar to that of No. 46206.

QUALITY OF GLAZE, poor ; colour, dull blue.

Two large fragments only.

46209. **Cylindrical Libation Vase** [9].—Blue glazed faïence.—Height 0 m ·11.—Maximum diameter 0 m ·115.—Room D.

Cylindrical libation vase, in blue glazed faïence, with ornamentation outlined in black.

ORNAMENTATION of *spherical top* and *bowl*, similar to that of No. 46206.

QUALITY OF GLAZE, thin and poor; colour, blue (much discoloured).

Parts of one side and top missing.

Stopper.—Blue glazed faïence.—Height 0 m ·05.—Diameter 0 m ·05.

In the shape of an inverted lotus flower, with rosette on the apex.

46210. **Cylindrical Libation Vase** [10].—Blue glazed faïence.—Height 0 m ·125.—Maximum diameter 0 m ·125.—Room D.

Cylindrical libation vase, in blue glazed faïence, with ornamentation outlined in black.

ORNAMENTATION of *spherical top*, similar to that of No. 46206.

Bowl, similar to that of No. 46206, except that around the circumference, at the base, is a row of rectangles, surmounted by a band of black dots.

QUALITY OF GLAZE, medium; colour, medium blue.

Broken into several pieces (two sides and part of top missing).

Stopper.—Blue glazed faïence.—Height 0 m ·05.—Diameter 0 m ·05.

Similar to that of No. 46206.

46211. **Cylindrical Libation Vase** [11].—Blue glazed faïence.—Height 0 m ·11.—Maximum diameter 0 m ·12.—Room D.

Cylindrical libation vase, in blue glazed faïence, with ornamentation outlined in black.

ORNAMENTATION of *spherical top* and *bowl*, similar to that of No. 46206.

QUALITY OF GLAZE, medium; colour, medium blue.

Broken into many pieces (part of top and sides missing).

46212. **Cylindrical Libation Vase** [12].—Blue glazed faïence.—Height 0 m ·12.—Maximum diameter 0 m ·12.—Room D.

Cylindrical libation vase, in blue glazed faïence, with ornamentation outlined in black.

ORNAMENTATION of *spherical top*, similar to that of No. 46206.

Bowl, around the circumference are three rows of zigzag lines, arranged vertically, and interrupted in the centre by the prenomen of Thoutmôsis IV, written in a rectangular panel. Around the circumference, at the bottom, is a band of rectangles.

QUALITY OF GLAZE, medium; colour, medium blue.

Broken into several pieces (parts missing).

Stopper.—Blue glazed faïence.—Height 0 m ·05.—Diameter 0 m ·05.

Similar to that of No. 46209.

46213. Cylindrical Libation Vase [13].—Blue glazed faïence.—Maximum diameter 0 m ·11.—Room D.

Cylindrical libation vase, in blue glazed faïence, with ornamentation outlined in black.

ORNAMENTATION of *spherical top* and *bowl*, similar to No. 46212.

QUALITY OF GLAZE, medium; colour, medium blue.

Broken (three pieces of the sides and bottom only).

46214. Cylindrical Libation Vase [14].—Blue glazed faïence.—Chamber 3.

Cylindrical libation vase, in blue glazed faïence, with ornamentation outlined in black.

ORNAMENTATION of *spherical top* and *bowl*, similar to No. 46212.

QUALITY OF GLAZE, medium; colour, medium blue.

Broken (fragments missing from top and sides).

46215. Cylindrical Libation Vase [15].—Blue glazed faïence.—Height 0 m ·12.—Diameter 0 m ·145.—Room D.

Cylindrical libation vase, in blue glazed faïence, with ornamentation outlined in black.

ORNAMENTATION of *spherical top*, similar to that of No. 46206.

Bowl, plain, except two lines running around the circumference at the top, and a thick line round the bottom.

QUALITY OF GLAZE, medium; colour, medium blue.

Nearly complete (fragment of side missing).

46216. Cylindrical Libation Vase [16].—Blue glazed faïence.—Height 0 m ·105.—Diameter 0 m ·14.—Room D.

Cylindrical libation vase, in blue glazed faïence, with ornamentation outlined in black.

ORNAMENTATION of *spherical top* and *bowl*, similar to that of No. 46215.

QUALITY OF GLAZE, medium; colour, medium blue.

Two-thirds of side wanting.

46217. Cylindrical Libation Vase [17].—Blue glazed faïence.—Maximum diameter 0 m ·125.—Room D.

Cylindrical libation vase, in blue glazed faïence, with ornamentation outlined in black.

ORNAMENTATION: *Spherical top*. Arranged around the opening is a row of rounded petals, alternating with sharply pointed ones. Outside this are (1) two black lines, (2) a broad plain blue band, and (3) two black lines.

Bowl, plain.

QUALITY OF GLAZE, medium; colour, medium blue.

Broken (pieces of top, bottom and sides missing).

46218. **Cylindrical Libation Vase** [18].—Blue glazed faïence.—Height 0 m ·12.—Maximum diameter 0 m ·10.—Room D.—Plate XX.

Cylindrical libation vase, in blue glazed faïence, with ornamentation outlined in black.

ORNAMENTATION : *Spherical top.* Around the opening is a narrow blue band and a row of short round-topped petals. Dividing the spherical top from the bowl are two black lines.

Bowl, similar to No. 46209.

QUALITY OF GLAZE, medium; colour, medium blue.

Broken. Fragment of bottom missing (otherwise complete).

Stopper.—Blue glazed faïence.—Height 0 m ·05.—Diameter 0 m ·05.

In the shape of an inverted lotus flower with hairy sepals, and a black spot on the apex. Very fine glaze.

Cylindrical Libation Vase [19].—Blue glazed faïence.—Height 0 m ·12.—Diameter 0 m ·10.—Chamber 3.

Cylindrical libation vase, in blue glazed faïence, with ornamentation outlined in black.

ORNAMENTATION of *spherical top* and *bowl*, similar to that of No. 18, except that the prenomen of Thoutmôsis IV is written in a cartouche, thus :—

QUALITY OF GLAZE, medium; colour, medium blue.

Broken into several pieces (bottom and parts of sides missing).

[Davis Collection.]

46219. **Cylindrical Libation Vase** [20].—Blue glazed faïence.—Height 0 m ·12.—Diameter 0 m ·10.—Room D.

Cylindrical libation vase, in blue glazed faïence, with ornamentation outlined in black.

ORNAMENTATION of *spherical top* and *bowl*, similar to No. [19].

QUALITY OF GLAZE, poor; colour, lightish blue.

Broken into several pieces; nearly complete.

Stopper.—Blue glazed faïence.—Height 0 m ·045.—Diameter 0 m ·045.

In the shape of an inverted lotus flower, with a black spot on the apex.

46220. **Cylindrical Libation Vase** [21].—Blue glazed faïence.—Diameter 0 m ·10.—Chambers 3 and 4.

Cylindrical libation vase, in blue glazed faïence, with ornamentation outlined in black.

ORNAMENTATION. *Spherical top* ; missing.

Bowl, similar to No. [19], except that the prenomen of Thoutmôsis IV is written between the scales of the pattern and not in a panel.

PLATE XX

46218ᴬ   [28ᴬ]

46218.   [28]

LIBATION VASES.

QUALITY OF GLAZE, medium; colour, medium blue.

Broken into several pieces.   (Spherical top and parts of sides missing.)

Stopper.—Blue glazed faïence.—Height 0 m ·045.—Diameter 0 m ·045.
Similar to that of No. 46219.

— **Cylindrical Libation Vase** [22].—Blue glazed faïence.—Diameter
0 m ·10.—Chamber 3.

Cylindrical libation vase, in blue glazed faïence, ornamented with designs outlined in
black.

ORNAMENTATION : *Spherical top*, similar to that of No. 46218.

Bowl, around the circumference are two bands of equal height of ornamentation,
consisting of (1) three rows of scales, and (2) a row of ☥-signs, alternating with
🪬-signs.   In the front of the bowl a vertical column interrupts this decoration : in
it is written the prenomen of Thoutmôsis IV, 𓇋𓏏𓇳𓍢𓆣𓏥𓊗.

QUALITY OF GLAZE, medium; colour, medium blue.

Eight pieces of the top and sides.

Stopper.—Blue glazed faïence.—Height 0 m ·045.—Diameter 0 m ·045.
Similar to that of No. 46220.

[Davis Collection.]

46221. Cylindrical Libation Vase [23].—Blue glazed faïence.—Height
0 m ·12.—Maximum diameter 0 m ·11.—Room D.

Cylindrical libation vase, in blue glazed faïence, ornamented with designs outlined in
black.

ORNAMENTATION : *Spherical top*.   Around the opening are two black lines, and the
remaining part is divided into four quarters by double vertical black lines, having a
row of dots on either side, and in the compartments thus formed are drawn in
outline lotus flowers, with pointed hairy sepals.   Separating the spherical top from
the bowl are two black lines.

Bowl, around the circumference at the top is a band composed of three rows of
scales, beneath which are double black lines.   Below this the circumference of the
bowl is divided into four plain panels, by double vertical lines continued from the
spherical top, with dots on either side.   Interrupting the designs on the bowl is a
column of hieroglyphs giving the prenomen of Thoutmôsis IV, 𓇋𓏏𓇳𓏜𓍢𓆣𓏥,
with double lines on either side.

Round the base of the bowl is a thick black line.

QUALITY OF GLAZE, medium; colour, medium blue.

Broken into several pieces (parts of sides and bottom missing).

46222. Spherical top of a cylindrical Libation Vase [24].—Blue glazed
faïence.—Diameter 0 m ·09.—Room D.

Spherical top of a cylindrical libation vase, in blue glazed faïence, with ornamentation
outlined in black.

ORNAMENTATION : An inverted lotus flower with narrow and pointed hairy sepals
and petals.

QUALITY OF GLAZE, medium ; colour, medium blue.

46223. Spherical top of a cylindrical Libation Vase [25].—Blue glazed
faïence.—Diameter 0 m ·09.—Chamber 3.

Spherical top of a cylindrical libation vase, in blue glazed faïence, with ornamentation
outlined in black.

ORNAMENTATION : An inverted lotus flower with pointed petals and sepals.

QUALITY OF GLAZE, medium ; colour, medium blue.

—   **Spherical top of a cylindrical Libation Vase** [26].—Blue glazed
faïence.—Diameter 0 m ·10.—Room D.

Spherical top of a cylindrical libation vase, in blue glazed faïence, with ornamentation
outlined in black.

ORNAMENTATION : Lotus flowers with hairy pointed sepals, alternating with lotus buds.

QUALITY OF GLAZE, medium ; colour, medium blue.

[Davis Collection.]

46224. Spherical top of a Cylindrical Libation Vase [27].—Blue glazed
faïence.—Diameter 0 m ·10.—Room D.

Spherical top of a cylindrical libation vase, in blue glazed faïence, with ornamentation
outlined in black.

ORNAMENTATION : Round the opening is a row of twelve round-topped petals, forming
a large rosette. Outside this is a curved line and a second row of short narrow
petals.

QUALITY OF GLAZE, medium ; colour, medium blue.

—   **Cylindrical Libation Vase** [28].—Blue glazed faïence.—Height
0 m ·10.—Diameter 0 m ·095.—Room D.—Plate XX [28, 28*a*].

Cylindrical libation vase, in blue glazed faïence, with ornamentation outlined in black.

ORNAMENTATION : *Spherical top*, plain.

Bowl, plain, except for a vertical line of hieroglyphs running down its centre, and
reading :

QUALITY OF GLAZE, medium ; colour, medium blue.

Broken into several pieces (nearly complete).

[Davis Collection.]

46225. Cylindrical Libation Vase [29].—Blue glazed faïence.—Height 0 m ·095.—Maximum diameter 0 m ·09.—Room D.

Cylindrical libation vase, in blue glazed faïence, with ornamentation outlined in black.

ORNAMENTATION of *spherical top* and *bowl*, similar to No. [28].

QUALITY OF GLAZE, medium ; colour, medium blue.

Broken into several pieces (nearly complete).

14. ⌀-SHAPED VASES.

46226.   Vase [1].—Blue glazed faïence.—Height 0 m ·26.—Maximum diameter 0 m ·07.—Room D.—Plate XXI.

⌀ –Shaped vase, in blue glazed faïence.

ORNAMENTATION in black outline : *Lip*, a thick black line runs around the rim.   *Neck*, a row of alternate ♀ and ⌘ signs.   *Bowl* (1) an inverted lotus flower, with sharply-pointed sepals and petals, the former lined to represent veining ; (2) front, a double column of hieroglyphs, reading : ⌗⌗⌗⌗⌗⌗⌗⌗⌗⌗⌗⌗⌗⌗⌗⌗⌗⌗. This double column is enclosed on either side by black vertical lines, and then, on the sides and back of the vase, are nine horizontal rows of scales alternately arranged ; (3) a band of rectangles.   *Foot* (1) five rows of zigzag lines ; (2) an inverted lotus flower, with sharply-pointed sepals and petals, the latter lined to represent veining ; (3) a thick black line runs around the rim.

QUALITY OF GLAZE, good ; colour, a medium blue.

Broken into four pieces (complete) ; the neck has been anciently mended.

Stopper.—Blue glazed faïence.—Height 0 m ·06.—Maximum diameter 0 m ·06.

In the form of an inverted lotus flower, with sepals and petals outlined in black.

QUALITY OF GLAZE, fair ; colour, a medium blue.

46227.   Fragments of a Vase [2].—Blue glazed faïence.—Room D.

Two pieces of a ⌀ –shaped vase, in blue glazed faïence ; the entire bowl wanting.

ORNAMENTATION : *Lip*, a thick black line runs around the rim.   *Neck*, a row of hieroglyphs.   *Foot*, similar to that of No. 46226.

QUALITY OF GLAZE, poor ; colour, medium blue.

Remains of papyrus strip bindings are still attached to the neck.

46228.   Fragments of a Vase [3].—Blue glazed faïence.—Room D.

Two pieces of a ⌀ –shaped vase, in blue glazed faïence ; the entire bowl wanting.

ORNAMENTATION : *Lip* and *neck*, similar to No. 46227.   *Foot*, similar to that of No. 46226.

QUALITY OF GLAZE, medium ; colour, medium blue.

Remains of papyrus strip bindings are still attached to the neck. The neck also shows traces of ancient mending.

PLATE XXI.

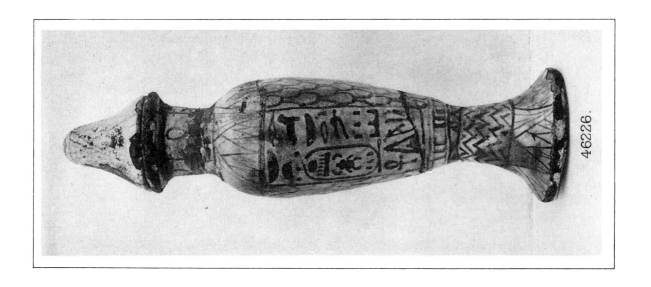

46226.

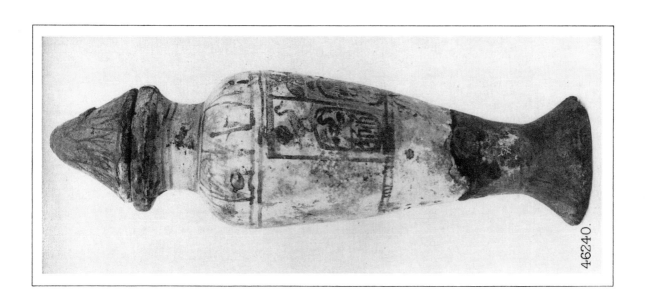

46240.

VASES.

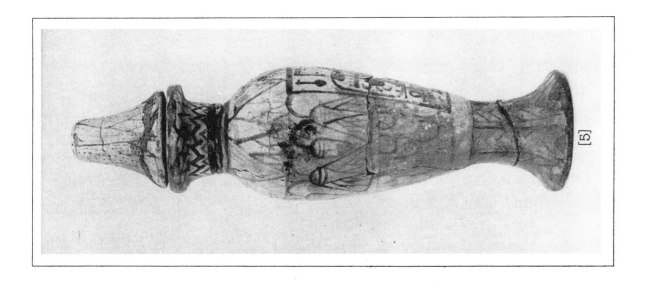

[5]

46229. **Foot of a Vase** [4].—Blue glazed faïence.—Room D.

Foot of a vase, in blue glazed faïence, with ornamentation similar to that of No. 46226.
QUALITY OF GLAZE, medium; colour, medium blue.

— **Vase** [5].—Blue glazed faïence.—Height 0 m ·255.—Maximum diameter 0 m ·075.—Room D.—Plate XXI [5].

〉–shaped vase, in blue glazed faïence.

ORNAMENTATION in black outline: *Lip,* a thick black line runs around the rim. *Neck,* three rows of zigzag lines, beneath which are three black lines running round the circumference. *Bowl* (1) an inverted lotus flower with pointed sepals and petals, the former lined to represent veining; (2) front, a double line of hieroglyphs, reading: ⸂[hieroglyphs]⸃.
This double column is enclosed on either side by black vertical lines, and then on the sides and back of the vase are (*a*) a band of lotus flowers alternating with lotus buds, both inverted, and (*b*) four rows of scales: (3) plain band of blue. *Foot,* seven vertical columns of zigzag lines, each column divided by double vertical lines. A thick black line runs round the rim of foot.

QUALITY OF GLAZE, very good; colour, medium blue.

Five pieces (incomplete).

Stopper.—Blue glazed faïence.—Height 0 m ·065.—Maximum diameter 0 m ·06.

In the form of an inverted lotus flower, with sepals and petals outlined in black, with at the top an eight-petaled rosette.

Remains of papyrus strip binding are attached to the stopper.

[Davis Collection.]

46230. **Fragments of a Vase** [6].—Blue glazed faïence.—Room D.

Two pieces of a 〉–shaped vase, in blue glazed faïence; the entire bowl missing.

ORNAMENTATION in black outline: *Lip,* a thick black line runs around the rim. *Neck,* a row of drop-shaped pendants. *Foot,* similar to that of No. [5].

QUALITY OF GLAZE, poor; colour, medium blue.

Remains of papyrus strip binding are still attached to the neck.

46231. **Foot of a Vase** [7].—Blue glazed faïence.—Room D.

Foot of a 〉–shaped vase, in blue glazed faïence.

ORNAMENTATION: Similar to that of No. [5].

QUALITY OF GLAZE, medium; colour, medium blue.

46232.   Foot of a Vase [8].—Blue glazed faïence.—Room D.

Form of a ⚱ -shaped vase, in blue glazed faïence.

ORNAMENTATION: Similar to that of No. [5].

QUALITY OF GLAZE, medium; colour, medium blue.

46233.   Foot of a Vase [9].—Blue glazed faïence.—Room D.

Foot of ⚱ -shaped vase, in blue glazed faïence.

ORNAMENTATION: Similar to that of No. [5].

QUALITY OF GLAZE, medium; colour, medium blue.

46234.   Foot of a Vase [10].—Blue glazed faïence.—Room D.

Foot of a ⚱ -shaped vase, in blue glazed faïence.

ORNAMENTATION: Similar to that of No. [5].

QUALITY OF GLAZE, medium; colour, medium blue.

46235.   Foot of a Vase [11].—Blue glazed faïence.—Room D.

Foot of a ⚱ -shaped vase, in blue glazed faïence.

ORNAMENTATION: Similar to that of No. [5].

QUALITY OF GLAZE, poor; colour, medium blue.

46236.   Vase [12].—Blue glazed faïence.—Height 0 m ·265.—Maximum diameter 0 m ·075.—Room D.

⚱ -shaped vase, in blue glazed faïence.

ORNAMENTATION in black outline: *Lip,* missing. *Neck,* three rows of scales. *Bowl,* (1) an inverted lotus flower, with sharply-pointed sepals and petals; (2) a plain and broad band with, in front, a double column of hieroglyphs, reading: [hieroglyphs]. This double column is enclosed on either side by black vertical lines; (3) a second plain band, divided from the upper one by a double black line, running round the circumference of the vase. At the base of this is a narrow row of diamond-shaped lozenges. *Foot,* an inverted lotus flower with sharply-pointed sepals and petals, the former lined to represent veining.

QUALITY OF GLAZE, good; colour, a medium blue.

Broken into several pieces, and with remains of ancient blue paste for mending.

46237. Fragments of a Vase [13].—Blue glazed faïence.—Room D.

Two pieces of a ⅄ -shaped vase, in blue glazed faïence ; the entire bowl wanting.

ORNAMENTATION in black outline : *Lip,* a thick black line runs around the rim. *Neck,* a row of pendent roundish petals. *Foot,* an inverted lotus flower, similar to No. 12.

QUALITY OF GLAZE, medium ; colour, medium blue.

Remains of a papyrus binding are still attached to the neck and foot.

46238. Fragments of a Vase [14].—Blue glazed faïence.—Room D.

Two pieces of the neck and foot of a vase, in blue glazed faïence ; the entire bowl wanting.

ORNAMENTATION : Similar to No. 46237.

QUALITY OF GLAZE, medium ; colour, medium blue.

Much destroyed.

46239. Vase [15].—Blue glazed faïence.—Height 0 m ·24.—Maximum diameter 0 m ·07.—Room D.

⅄ -shaped vase, in blue glazed faïence, with ornamentation in black outline.

ORNAMENTATION : *Lip,* wanting. *Neck,* a row of drop-shaped pendants. *Bowl,* running round the upper part are (1) two black lines, (2) a narrow zigzag line, (3) two black lines, and (4) a band of rectangles. Beneath this is a broad band of lotus petals in black, then a narrow double row of rectangles, and a narrow band of semicircles outlined in black. The lower part of the bowl is plain save for double lines running round the centre. Interrupting these double lines on one side is the prenomen of Thouthmôsis IV, written in a cartouche within a rectangular panel. *Foot,* an inverted lotus flower with dotted sepals.

QUALITY OF GLAZE, good ; colour, medium blue.

Complete, save for the lip, which is wanting.

46240. Vase [16].—Blue glazed faïence.—Height 0 m ·27.—Maximum diameter, 0 m ·09.—Room D.—Plate XXI.

⅄ -shaped vase, in blue glazed faïence, with ornamentation in black outline.

ORNAMENTATION : *Lip,* a thick black line runs around the rim. *Neck,* plain save for double lines running round top and bottom. *Bowl,* (1) a row of inverted lotus petals and sepals, (2) a double black line, (3) a plain band of blue, with, on the front, the nomen and prenomen of Thoutmôsis IV, written within a rectangular panel surmounted by a ⊏⊐ -sign. At the base of this panel is a double line enclosing a row of rectangles, which runs right round the circumference of the bowl. (4) A plain band. *Foot*, an inverted lotus flower with sharply pointed petals.

QUALITY OF GLAZE, good; colour, medium blue, discoloured in places.

Broken into three pieces (complete) and anciently mended.

Stopper.—Blue glazed faïence.—Height 0 m ·06.—Maximum diameter 0 m ·065.

In the form of an inverted lotus flower.

46241. Fragments of a Vase [17].—Blue glazed faïence.—Room D.

Four pieces of a ⏳ -shaped vase, in blue glazed faïence, with ornamentation in black outline.

ORNAMENTATION: *Lip*, rim, black. *Neck*, plain save for a double line running round the circumferences at the centre. Separating the neck from the bowl are three black lines. *Bowl*, (1) a row of inverted lotus petals, (2) a broad blue band with, on the front of the vase, the following inscription, enclosed in a rectangular panel :—

Foot, an inverted lotus flower with sharply-pointed petals.

QUALITY OF GLAZE, medium; colour, medium blue.

46242. Foot of a Vase [18].—Blue glazed faïence.—Room D.

Foot of a ⏳ -shaped vase, in blue glazed faïence.

ORNAMENTATION: similar to that of No. 46241.

QUALITY OF GLAZE, medium; colour, medium blue.

Broken into two pieces: anciently mended.

46243. Foot of a Vase [19].—Blue glazed faïence.—Room D.

Foot of a ⏳ -shaped vase, in blue glazed faïence.

ORNAMENTATION: similar to that of No. 46241.

QUALITY OF GLAZE, medium; colour, medium blue.

46244. Vase [20].—Blue glazed faïence.—Height 0 m ·185.—Maximum diameter 0 m ·06.—Room D.—Plate XXII.

⏳ -shaped vase, in blue glazed faïence, with ornamentation in black outline.

ORNAMENTATION: *Lip*, a band of black runs around the rim. *Neck*, plain. *Bowl*, without ornamentation, but inscribed in the front with the prenomen of Thoutmôsis IV, enclosed in a rectangular panel. *Foot*, a band of black runs around the rim.

PLATE XXII.

VASES.

46267.

46257.

46244.

46253.

QUALITY OF GLAZE, poor; colour, pale blue.

Broken into two pieces (complete).

Stopper.—Blue glazed faïence.—Height 0 m ·04.—Maximum diameter 0 m ·05.

In the form of an inverted lotus flower, but without ornamentation.

— **Vase** [21].—Blue glazed faïence.—Height 0 m ·185.—Maximum diameter 0 m ·06.—Room D.

⦚ –shaped vase, in blue glazed faïence, with ornamentation similar to that of No. 46244.

QUALITY OF GLAZE, poor; colour, pale blue.

Broken, but complete.

Bears remains of papyrus binding on the neck and stopper.

Stopper.—Blue glazed faïence.—Height 0 m ·04.—Maximum diameter 0 m ·05.

In the form of an inverted lotus flower, but without ornamentation.

[Davis Collection.]

46245. Vase [22].—Blue glazed faïence.—Height 0 m ·185.—Maximum diameter 0 m ·06.—Room D.

⦚ –shaped vase, in blue glazed faïence, with ornamentation similar to that of No. 46244.

QUALITY OF GLAZE, poor; colour, medium blue.

Stopper.—Blue glazed faïence.—Height 0 m ·035.—Maximum diameter 0 m ·045.

In the form of an inverted lotus flower, without ornamentation.

46246. Vase [23].—Blue glazed faïence.—Height 0 m ·185.—Maximum diameter 0 m ·06.—Chamber 3.

⦚ –shaped vase, in blue glazed faïence, with ornamentation similar to that of No. 46244.

QUALITY OF GLAZE, poor; colour, medium blue.

Three pieces; lower part of bowl wanting.

Stopper.—Blue glazed faïence.—Height 0 m ·035.—Maximum diameter 0 m ·045.

In the form of an inverted lotus flower, without ornamentation.

46247. Vase [24].—Blue glazed faïence.—Height 0 m ·185.—Maximum diameter 0 m ·06.—Room D.

⦚ –shaped vase, in blue glazed faïence, with ornamentation similar to that of No. 46244.

QUALITY OF GLAZE, poor, badly discoloured; colour, medium blue.

Complete.

46248. Vase [25].—Blue glazed faïence.—Height 0 m ·18. Maximum diameter 0 m ·06.—Room D.

☥ –shaped vase, in blue glazed faïence, with ornamentation similar to that of No. 46244.

QUALITY OF GLAZE, poor; colour, medium blue.

Remains of papyrus binding on foot and round neck.

46249. Vase [26].—Blue glazed faïence.—Height 0 m ·18.—Maximum diameter 0 m ·06.—Room D.

☥ –shaped vase, in blue glazed faïence, with ornamentation similar to that of No. 46244.

QUALITY OF GLAZE, poor; colour, medium blue.

46250. Vase [27].—Blue glazed faïence.—Height 0 m ·18.—Maximum diameter 0 m ·055.—Room D.

☥ –shaped vase, in blue glazed faïence, with ornamentation similar to that of No. 46244.

QUALITY OF GLAZE, poor; colour, medium blue.

Remains of papyrus binding on foot and around neck.

46251. Foot of a Vase [28].—Blue glazed faïence.—Room D.

Foot of a ☥ –shaped vase, in blue glazed faïence, similar to that of No. 46244.

QUALITY OF GLAZE, poor; colour, medium blue.

46252. Foot of a Vase [29].—Blue glazed faïence.—Room D.

Foot of a ☥ –shaped vase, in blue glazed faïence, similar to that of No. 46244.

QUALITY OF GLAZE, poor; colour, medium blue.

46253. Vase [30].—Blue glazed faïence.—Height 0 m ·15.—Maximum diameter 0 m ·06.—Room D.—Plate XXII.

☥ –shaped vase, in blue glazed faïence, with ornamentation in black.

ORNAMENTATION: *Lip*, a thick black line runs around the rim. *Neck*, plain. *Bowl*, (1) a row of inverted lotus petals, (2) and (3) bands of plain blue divided by double black lines. On the front of band 2 is a rectangular panel enclosing the prenomen of Thoutmôsis IV, (cartouche). *Foot*, an inverted lotus flower.

QUALITY OF GLAZE, poor, and much stained; colour, medium blue.

Stopper.—Blue glazed faïence.—Height 0 m ·04.—Maximum diameter 0 m ·045.

In the form of an inverted lotus flower.

46254. **Vase** [31].—Blue glazed faïence.—Height 0 m ·165.—Maximum diameter 0 m ·06.—Room D.

⑂ –shaped vase, in blue glazed faïence, with ornamentation in black.

ORNAMENTATION: *Lip*, plain. *Neck*, a single line runs around the circumference in the middle. *Bowl*, divided into four broad bands by double lines running round it; in the upper band is a row of drop-shaped pendants; the lower three bands are plain. *Foot*, plain.

QUALITY OF GLAZE, poor; colour, medium blue.

46255. **Vase** [32].—Blue glazed faïence.—Height 0 m ·165.—Maximum diameter 0 m ·06.—Room D.

⑂ –shaped vase, in blue glazed faïence, with ornamention in black.

ORNAMENTATION: *Lip*, wanting. *Neck*, plain. *Bowl*, divided into three broad bands by double lines running round it; in the upper band is a row of elongated papyrus petals; the lower two bands are plain. *Foot*, plain.

QUALITY OF GLAZE, poor; colour, medium blue.

Lip broken off.

46256. **Foot of a Vase** [33].—Blue glazed faïence.—Room D.

Foot of a ⑂ –shaped vase, similar to that of No. 46255.

QUALITY OF GLAZE, poor; colour, medium blue.

46257. **Vase** [34].—Blue glazed faïence.—Height 0 m ·175.—Maximum diameter 0 m ·065.—Room D.—Plate XXII.

⑂ –shaped vase, in blue glazed faïence, with ornamentation in black.

ORNAMENTATION: *Lip*, around its circumference is a row of dots, with a double line beneath. *Neck*, plain. *Bowl*, at the top is a band, separated from the neck above by a double line and from the lower part of the bowl by a single line, composed of a series of vertical straight lines alternating with vertical zigzag lines. Below this band the bowl is plain, save for a vertical column of hieroglyphs running down the front, and reading: ⦿. *Foot*, a broad band, divided from the bowl above by double lines, and from the rim below by double lines, enclosing a series of vertical straight lines alternating with vertical zigzag lines.

QUALITY OF GLAZE, medium ; colour, lightish blue.

Broken into three pieces (complete).

Stopper.—Blue glazed faïence.—Height 0 m ·05.—Maximum diameter 0 m ·05.—
Room D.

Bell-shaped stopper, in blue glazed faïence, ornamented in black. At the top are four
lines running round its circumference ; the centre part is plain, while below is a
band composed of a row of drop-shaped pendants hanging from a double line.

QUALITY OF GLAZE, medium ; colour, lightish blue.

— **Vase** [35].—Blue glazed faïence.—Height 0 m ·17.—Maximum
diameter 0 m ·06.—Room D.

𓊖 –shaped vase, in blue glazed faïence, with ornamentation in black.

ORNAMENTATION : *Lip* and *neck*, plain. *Bowl*, at the top is a band, separated from the
neck above and from the lower part of the bowl by single lines, composed of a
row of double vertical lines enclosing long, drop-shaped pendants. Below this band
the bowl is plain, save for a vertical column of hieroglyphs on its front, similar to
that on No. 46257. *Foot*, an inverted lotus flower, with curved lines between the
tips of the petals.

QUALITY OF GLAZE, medium ; colour, medium blue.

Stopper.—Blue glazed faïence.—Height 0 m ·04.—Maximum diameter 0 m ·045.—
Room D.

Bell-shaped stopper, in blue glazed faïence, ornamented with a row of nine long, drop-
shaped pendants, suspended from three lines running around the top.

[Davis Collection.]

46258. **Vase** [36].—Blue glazed faïence.—Height 0 m ·165.—Diameter
0 m ·06.—Room D.

𓊖 –shaped vase, in blue glazed faïence, with ornamentation in black.

ORNAMENTATION : *Lip*, plain. *Neck*, plain, but divided from the rim and bowl by
double lines. *Bowl*, around the top is a row of drop-shaped pendants, suspended
from the lower line of the neck. Below this row the bowl is plain, save for a
vertical column of hieroglyphs on its front, similar to that of No. 46257. *Foot*,
similar to that of No. [35].

QUALITY OF GLAZE, medium ; colour, medium blue.

46259. **Fragments of a Vase** [37].—Blue glazed faïence.—Room D.

Two fragments of the neck and foot of a 𓊖 –shaped vase, in blue glazed faïence, with
ornamentation in black.

ORNAMENTATION: *Neck*, similar to that of No. 46257. *Foot*, a row of straight lines arranged vertically, enclosing a row of dots between every other line.

QUALITY OF GLAZE, medium; colour, medium blue.

46260. Foot of a Vase [38].—Blue glazed faïence.—Room D.

Foot of a 𝖮 –shaped vase, similar to that of No. 46257.

46261. Foot of a Vase [39].—Blue glazed faïence.—Room D.

Foot of a 𝖮 –shaped vase, similar to that of No. 46259.

46262. Vase [40].—Blue glazed faïence.—Height 0 m ·16.—Maximum diameter 0 m ·06.—Room D.

𝖮 –shaped vase, in blue glazed faïence, with ornamentation in black.

ORNAMENTATION: *Lip*, plain. *Neck*, plain, but divided from the rim and bowl by double lines. *Bowl*, at the top is a row of small drop-shaped pendants, suspended from the lower line of the neck. Below this is a line running horizontally round the bowl just above its maximum circumference. Beneath it is plain, save for a vertical column of hieroglyphs on its front, similar to that of No. 34. *Foot*, divided from the bowl above by a double line, from the lower one of which is suspended a row of drop-shaped pendants, which extend to midway down the front; then comes (1) a black line running horizontally round it, (2) a plain band, and (3) a row of ᴀᴀᴀᴀᴀ immediately above the rim of the foot.

QUALITY OF GLAZE, medium; colour, medium blue.

46263. Foot of a Vase [41].—Blue glazed faïence.—Room D.

Foot of a 𝖮 –shaped vase, similar to that of No. 46262.

46264. Vase [42].—Blue glazed faïence.—Height 0 m ·165.—Diameter 0 m ·06.—Room D.

𝖮 –shaped vase, in blue glazed faïence, with ornamentation similar to that of No. 46262, except that the ᴀᴀᴀᴀᴀ decoration is wanting from the foot.

QUALITY OF GLAZE, medium; colour, medium blue.

Stopper.—Blue glazed faïence.—Height 0 m ·165.—Maximum diameter 0 m ·06.—Room D.

Bell-shaped stopper with ornamentation similar to that of No. 46257.

46265. Fragments of a Vase [43].—Blue glazed faïence.—Room D.

Two fragments of the neck and foot of a 🝔 –shaped vase, in blue glazed faïence, with ornamentation similar to that of No. 46264.

QUALITY OF GLAZE, medium; colour, medium blue.

46266. Fragments of a Vase [44].—Blue glazed faïence.—Room D.

Two fragments of the neck and foot of a 🝔 –shaped vase, in blue glazed faïence, with ornamentation similar to that of No. 46264.

46267. Vase [45].—Blue glazed faïence.—Height 0 m ·15.—Maximum diameter 0 m ·065.—Room D.—Plate XXII.

🝔 –shaped vase, in blue glazed faïence, with ornamentation in black.

ORNAMENTATION : *Lip*, a thick black line runs around it. *Neck*, divided from the lip above and from the bowl below by a horizontal line running round its circumference; within the band thus formed are seven double lines arranged at equal distances from one another. *Bowl*, at the top is a row of inverted lotus petals, extending nearly halfway down the bowl. Around the circumference, at the centre of the bowl and again at the bottom of the bowl, are double lines enclosing a row of black and blue rectangles, while in the broad plain band between is the prenomen of Thoutmôsis IV, written vertically between the vertical lines. *Foot*, an inverted lotus flower.

QUALITY OF GLAZE, medium; colour, medium blue.

Broken (incomplete).

Stopper.—Blue glazed faïence.—Height 0 m ·04.—Maximum diameter 0 m ·05.

Bell-shaped stopper in blue glazed faïence without ornamentation.

46268. Vase [46].—Blue glazed faïence.—Height 0 m ·165.—Maximum diameter 0 m ·065.— Found in well.

🝔 –shaped vase, in blue glazed faïence, with ornamentation in black outline.

ORNAMENTATION : *Lip*, plain. *Neck*, divided from the lip and bowl by a horizontal line running round its circumference : within the band thus formed is a row of vertical lines, alternating with zigzag lines vertically arranged, *Bowl*, at the top is a row of drop-shaped pendants with a curved line below them. At the greatest diameter of the bowl is a horizontal double line, while another double line runs round the bottom of it : the broad band between is plain save for the prenomen of Thoutmôsis IV, which is written on the front of the vase between double vertical lines. *Foot*, seven double lines arranged at equal distances from one another.

QUALITY OF GLAZE, medium; colour, medium blue.

46269. Vase [47].—Blue glazed faïence.—Maximum diameter 0 m ·065.—Room D.

⍭ –shaped vase, in blue glazed faïence, with ornamentation in black outline.

ORNAMENTATION: *Lip*, rim, black. *Neck*, upper part, plain; a row of spots between the horizontal lines around the bottom. *Bowl*, at the top is a row of drop-shaped pendants, with a curved line below them. A little below the greatest diameter of the bowl is a horizontal double line, with zigzag line between. The lower half of the bowl is similar to that of No. 46268. *Foot*, similar to that of No. 46268.

Three pieces (incomplete).

QUALITY OF GLAZE, medium; colour, medium blue.

46270. Fragments of a Vase [48].—Blue glazed faïence.—Room D.

Two fragments of the neck and foot of a ⍭ –shaped vase, in blue glazed faïence, with ornamentation in black outline.

ORNAMENTATION: *Neck*, similar to that of No. 46269. *Foot*, an inverted lotus flower with hairy sepals.

QUALITY OF GLAZE, medium; colour, medium blue.

46271. Fragments of a Vase [49].—Blue glazed faïence.—Room D.

Two fragments of the neck and foot of a ⍭ –shaped vase, in blue glazed faïence, with ornamentation in black outline.

ORNAMENTATION: Similar to that of No. 46270.

QUALITY OF GLAZE, medium; colour, medium blue.

46272. Foot of a Vase [50].—Blue glazed faïence.—Room D.

Foot of a ⍭ –shaped vase, similar to that of No. 46270.

QUALITY OF GLAZE, medium; colour, medium blue.

46273. Foot of a Vase [51].—Blue glazed faïence.—Room D.

Foot of a ⍭ –shaped vase, similar to that of No. 46267.

QUALITY OF GLAZE, medium; colour, medium blue.

46274. Fragment of foot of a Vase [52].—Blue glazed faïence.—Room D.

Fragment of the foot of a ⍭ –shaped vase, similar to that of No. 46270.

QUALITY OF GLAZE, medium; colour, medium blue.

46275. Fragment of a Vase [53].—Blue glazed faïence.—Maximum diameter 0 m ·06.—Room D.

Fragment of the upper part of a ⌀ -shaped vase, similar to that of No. 46269.

QUALITY OF GLAZE, medium ; colour, medium blue.

46276. Fragment of a Vase [54].—Blue glazed faïence.—Diameter 0 m ·06. —Room D.

Fragment of the upper part of a ⌀ -shaped vase, similar to No. 46268.

QUALITY OF GLAZE, medium ; colour, medium blue.

46277. Neck of a Vase [55].—Blue glazed faïence.—Room D.

Neck of a ⌀ -shaped vase, similar to No. 46267.

QUALITY OF GLAZE, poor ; colour, medium blue.

46278. Fragment of a Vase [56].—Blue glazed faïence.—Room D.

Fragment of the lower part of a ⌀ -shaped vase, in blue glazed faïence, with ornamentation in black.

ORNAMENTATION : *Bowl*, rows of scales, having a black spot at base. *Foot*, a row of inverted and long pointed lotus petals.

QUALITY OF GLAZE, good ; colour, a fine rich blue.

46279. Fragments of a Vase [57].—Blue glazed faïence.—Room D.

Two fragments of a ⌀ -shaped vase, in blue glazed faïence, with ornamentation in black.

ORNAMENTATION : *Bowl*, running round the top is a black line, separating it from the neck, and to this line is suspended a row of long, drop-shaped pendants, with a wavy line below. A black line separates this upper band from the lower half of the bowl and foot, which is ornamented with rows of large scales having a black spot at the base of each.

QUALITY OF GLAZE, good ; colour, a fine blue.

46280. Fragment of a Vase [58].—Blue glazed faïence.—Maximum diameter 0 m ·06.—Room D.

Fragment of the upper part of a ⌀ -shaped vase, in blue glazed faïence, similar, with ornamentation in black.

ORNAMENTATION: *Neck*, around it are seven double vertical lines arranged at equal distances from one another. *Bowl*, running round the top is a black line separating it from the neck, and to this line is suspended a row of drop-shaped pendants, with a curved line below. A black line separates this upper band from the lower half of the bowl, which is ornamented with inverted lotus petals.

QUALITY OF GLAZE, medium ; colour, medium blue.

46281. Fragment of a Vase [59].—Blue glazed faïence.—Maximum diameter 0 m ·06.—Room D.

Fragment of the upper part of a ⦵ -shaped vase, in blue glazed faïence, with ornamentation in black.

ORNAMENTATION : *Lip*, rim, black. *Neck*, around the circumference are vertical lines alternating with lotus petals in full black. *Bowl*, running round the top is a black line separating it from the neck, and below, covering the upper half of the bowl, is a row of long and pointed inverted lotus petals in full black.

QUALITY OF GLAZE, medium ; colour, medium blue.

46282. Foot of a Vase [60].—Blue glazed faïence.—Room D.

Foot of a ⦵ -shaped vase, in blue glazed faïence, of a similar shape to No. 46278, but without ornamentation.

QUALITY OF GLAZE, medium ; colour, medium blue.

15. STOPPERS OF VASES.

46283. Stopper of a Vase [1].—Blue glazed faïence.—Height 0 m ·06.—Maximum diameter 0 m ·06.—Chamber 3.

In the form of an inverted lotus flower, with sepals and petals outlined in black.
QUALITY OF GLAZE, bad; colour, medium blue.

46284. Stopper of a Vase [2].—Blue glazed faïence.—Height 0 m ·05.—Maximum diameter 0 m ·06.—Room D.

Form and ornamentation similar to No. 46283.
QUALITY OF GLAZE, bad; colour, medium blue.

46285. Stopper of a Vase [3].—Blue glazed faïence.—Height 0 m ·06.—Maximum diameter 0 m ·065.—Room D.

Form and ornamentation similar to No. 46283.
QUALITY OF GLAZE, medium; colour, medium blue.

46286. Stopper of a Vase [4].—Blue glazed faïence.—Height 0 m ·06.—Maximum diameter 0 m ·07.—Room D.

Form and ornamentation similar to No. 46283.
QUALITY OF GLAZE, medium; colour, medium blue.

46287. Stopper of a Vase [5].—Blue glazed faïence.—Height 0 m ·05.—Maximum diameter 0 m ·06.—Chamber 3.

In the form of an inverted lotus flower, with a black line running round its greatest diameter.
QUALITY OF GLAZE, good; colour, medium blue.

46288. Stopper of a Vase [6].—Blue glazed faïence.—Height 0 m ·05.—Maximum diameter 0 m ·055.—Room D.

Form and ornamentation similar to No. 46287.
QUALITY OF GLAZE, good; colour, medium blue.

46289. **Stopper of a Vase** [7].—Blue glazed faïence.—Height 0 m ·05.— Maximum diameter 0 m ·055.—Room D.

Form and ornamentation similar to No. 46287.

QUALITY OF GLAZE, good; colour, medium blue.

46290. **Stopper of a Vase** [8].—Blue glazed faïence.—Height 0 m ·05.— Maximum diameter 0 m ·055.—Room D.

Form and ornamentation similar to No. 46287.

QUALITY OF GLAZE, good; colour, medium blue.

46291. **Stopper of a Vase** [9].—Blue glazed faïence.—Height 0 m ·05.— Maximum diameter 0 m ·05.—Room D.

Form and ornamentation similar to No. 46287.

QUALITY OF GLAZE, medium; colour, medium blue.

46292. **Stopper of a Vase** [10].—Blue glazed faïence.—Height 0 m ·05.— Maximum diameter 0 m ·055.—Chamber 3.

Form and ornamentation similar to No. 46287.

QUALITY OF GLAZE, medium; colour, medium blue.

46293. **Stopper of a Vase** [11].—Blue glazed faïence.—Height 0 m ·05.— Maximum diameter 0 m ·055.—Room D.

Form and ornamentation similar to No. 46287.

QUALITY OF GLAZE, medium; colour, medium blue.

46294. **Stopper of a Vase** [12].—Blue glazed faïence.—Height 0 m ·05.— Maximum diameter 0 m ·05.—Room D.

Form of ornamentation similar to No. 46287.

QUALITY OF GLAZE, medium; colour, medium blue.

46295. **Stopper of a Vase** [13].—Blue glazed faïence.—Height 0 m ·045.— Maximum diameter 0 m ·055.—Room D.

Form and ornamentation similar to No. 46287.

QUALITY OF GLAZE, medium; colour, medium blue.

11.

46296. Stopper of a Vase [14].—Blue glazed faïence.—Height 0 m ·05.—
Maximum diameter 0 m ·055.—Room D.

Form and ornamentation similar to No. 46287.

Quality of Glaze, medium; colour, medium blue.

46297. Stopper of a Vase [15].—Blue glazed faïence.—Height 0 m ·045.—
Maximum diameter 0 m ·05.—Room D.

Form and ornamentation similar to No. 46287.

Quality of Glaze, medium; colour, medium blue.

46298. Stopper of a Vase [16].—Blue glazed faïence.—Height 0 m ·04.—
Maximum diameter 0 m ·05.—Room D.

Form and ornamentation similar to No. 46287.

Quality of Glaze, medium; colour, medium blue.

46299. Stopper of a Vase [17].—Blue glazed faïence.—Height 0 m ·05.—
Maximum diameter 0 m ·06.—Room D.

Form and ornamentation similar to No. 46287.

Quality of Glaze, medium; colour, medium blue.

46300. Stopper of a Vase [18].—Blue glazed faïence.—Height 0 m ·05.—
Maximum diameter 0 m ·055.—Room D.

Form and ornamentation similar to No. 46287.

Quality of Glaze, medium; colour, medium blue.

—   **Stopper of a Vase** [19].—Blue glazed faïence.—Height 0 m ·04.—
Maximum diameter 0 m ·04.—Room D.

Form and ornamentation similar to No. 46287.

Quality of Glaze, medium; colour, medium blue.

[Davis Collection.]

—   **Stopper of a Vase** [20].—Blue glazed faïence.—Height 0 m ·04.—
Maximum diameter 0 m ·045.—Room D.

Form and ornamentation similar to No. 46287.

Quality of Glaze, rough; colour, medium blue.

[Davis Collection.]

46301. **Stopper of a Vase** [21].—Blue glazed faïence.—Height 0 m ·04.—Maximum diameter 0 m ·06.—Room D.

In the form of an inverted lotus flower, with petals and sepals outlined in black, and a black line around its greatest diameter.

QUALITY OF GLAZE, very poor; colour, dark blue.

A strip of papyrus pith is bound round the end of the stopper.

46302. **Stopper of a Vase** [22].—Blue glazed faïence.—Height 0 m ·05.—Maximum diameter 0 m ·06.—Room D.

In the form of an inverted lotus flower, with petals and sepals outlined in violet. Dots representing hairs are painted on the sepals, and a black line runs round its greatest diameter.

QUALITY OF GLAZE, good; colour, light blue.

— **Stopper of a Vase** [23].—Blue glazed faïence.—Height 0 m ·045.—Maximum diameter 0 m ·055.—Chamber 3.

In the form of an inverted lotus flower, with petals and sepals outlined in violet, and two violet lines painted round the top of the flower.

QUALITY OF GLAZE, medium (rough); colour medium blue.

[Davis Collection.]

46303. **Stopper of a Vase** [24].—Blue glazed faïence.—Height 0 m ·045.—Maximum diameter 0 m ·05.—Room D.

In the form of an inverted lotus flower, with sepals outlined in violet and dotted to represent hairs.

QUALITY OF GLAZE, good; colour medium blue.

46304. **Stopper of a Vase** [25].—Blue glazed faïence.—Height 0 m ·05.—Maximum diameter 0 m ·05.—Room D.

In the form of an inverted lotus flower, with sepals faintly outlined in violet.

QUALITY OF GLAZE, medium; colour, light blue.

A strip of papyrus pith is bound round the end of the stopper.

46305. **Stopper of a Vase** [26].—Blue glazed faïence.—Height 0 m ·04.—Maximum diameter 0 m ·05.—Room D.

In the form of an inverted lotus flower, with petals and sepals outlined in violet (very faint).

QUALITY OF GLAZE, medium; colour, darkish blue.

A strip of papyrus pith is bound round the end of the stopper.

—   **Stopper of a Vase** [27].—Blue glazed faïence.—Height 0 m ·05.
Maximum diameter 0 m ·055.—Room D.

In the form of an inverted lotus flower, with petals and sepals outlined in black; the
sepals dotted to represent hairs.

QUALITY OF GLAZE, poor; colour, very pale blue.

[Davis Collection.]

46306.   **Stopper of a Vase** [28].—Blue glazed faïence.—Height 0 m ·05.—
Maximum diameter 0 m ·05.—Room D.

In the form of an inverted lotus flower, with petals and sepals outlined in black; the
sepals dotted to represent hairs.

QUALITY OF GLAZE, good; colour, light blue.

46307.   **Stopper of a Vase** [29].—Blue glazed faïence.—Height 0 m ·04.—
Maximum diameter 0 m ·045.—Room D.

In the form of an inverted lotus flower, with sepals outlined in violet and dotted to
represent hairs.

QUALITY OF GLAZE, poor; colour, medium blue.

46308.   **Stopper of a Vase** [30].—Blue glazed faïence.—Height 0 m ·045.—
Maximum diameter 0 m ·05.—Room D.

In the form of an inverted lotus flower, with sepals roughly outlined in black.

QUALITY OF GLAZE, good; colour, medium blue.

46309.   **Stopper of a Vase** [31].—Blue glazed faïence.—Height 0 m ·05.—
Maximum diameter 0 m ·05.—Room D.

In the form of an inverted lotus flower, with sepals roughly outlined in greyish-black.

QUALITY OF GLAZE, good; colour, medium blue.

The end of the stopper is chipped off.

46310.   **Stopper of a Vase** [32].—Blue glazed faïence.—Height 0 m ·04.—
Maximum diameter 0 m ·05.—Room D.

Form and ornamentation similar to No. 46310.

QUALITY OF GLAZE, good; colour, medium blue.

46311. **Stopper of a Vase** [33].—Blue glazed faïence.—Height 0 m ·04.—Maximum diameter 0 m ·04.—Room **D.**

In the form of an inverted lotus flower, with sepals outlined in black, and dotted to represent hairs.

QUALITY OF GLAZE, good; colour, medium blue.

46312. **Stopper of a Vase** [34].—Blue glazed faïence.—Height 0 m ·045.—Maximum diameter 0 m ·045.—Room **D.**

Form and ornamentation similar to No. 46312.

QUALITY OF GLAZE, good; colour, medium blue.

46313. **Stopper of a Vase** [35].—Blue glazed faïence.—Height 0 m ·04.—Maximum diameter 0 m ·045.—Room **D.**

Form and ornamentation similar to No. 46312.

QUALITY OF GLAZE, good; colour, medium blue.

46314. **Stopper of a Vase** [36].—Blue glazed faïence.—Height 0 m ·04.—Maximum diameter 0 m ·045.—Room **D.**

Form and ornamentation similar to No. 46312.

QUALITY OF GLAZE, good; colour, medium blue.

46315. **Stopper of a Vase** [37].—Blue glazed faïence.—Height 0 m ·035.—Maximum diameter 0 m ·04.—Room **D.**

In the form of an inverted lotus flower, with ornamentation of thick twisted black lines.

QUALITY OF GLAZE, good; colour, dark blue.

— **Stopper of a Vase** [38].—Blue glazed faïence.—Height 0 m ·04.—Maximum diameter 0 m ·045.—Room **D.**

In the form of an inverted lotus flower, with ornamentation in very faint grey lines.

QUALITY OF GLAZE, good; colour, a fine medium blue.

The end of the stopper is broken off.

[Davis Collection.]

—   **Stopper of a Vase** [39].—Blue glazed faïence.—Height 0 m ·04.—
      Maximum diameter 0 m ·04.—Room D.

Form and ornamentation similar to No. 46312.

QUALITY OF GLAZE, good ; colour, medium blue.

[Davis Collection.]

—   **Stopper of a Vase** [40].—Blue glazed faïence.—Height 0 m ·04.—
      Maximum diameter 0 m ·04.—Room D.

Form and ornamentation similar to No. 46312.

QUALITY OF GLAZE, good ; colour, medium blue.

The end of the stopper is broken off.

[Davis Collection.]

—   **Stopper of a Vase** [41].—Blue glazed faïence.—Height 0 m ·04.—
      Maximum diameter 0 m ·045.—Room D.

In form of an inverted lotus flower, without ornamentation.

QUALITY OF GLAZE, poor ; colour, dark blue.

[Davis Collection.]

—   **Stopper of a Vase** [42].—Blue glazed faïence.—Height 0 m ·04.—
      Maximum diameter 0 m ·045.—Room D.

Form and ornamentation similar to No. 46312.

QUALITY OF GLAZE, medium ; colour, medium blue.

[Davis Collection.]

—   **Stopper of a Vase** [43].—Blue glazed faïence.—Height 0 m ·045.—
      Maximum diameter 0 m ·05.—Room D.

In the form of an inverted lotus flower, with petals and sepals outlined in black, and
four rings in black round the calyx of the flower.

QUALITY OF GLAZE, good ; colour, dark blue.

The end of the stopper is broken.

[Davis Collection.]

—   **Stopper of a Vase** [44].—Blue glazed faïence.—Height 0 m ·045.—
      Maximum diameter 0 m ·05.—Room D.

Form and ornamentation similar to No. [43].

QUALITY OF GLAZE, good ; colour, dark blue.

[Davis Collection.]

— **Stopper of a Vase** [45].—Blue glazed faïence.—Height 0 m ·045.—
Maximum diameter 0 m ·05.—Room D.

Form and ornamentation similar to No. [43].

QUALITY OF GLAZE, good ; colour, dark blue.

[Davis Collection.]

— **Stopper of a Vase** [46].—Blue glazed faïence.—Height 0 m ·045.—
Maximum diameter 0 m ·05.—Chamber 3.

Form and ornamentation similar to No. [43].

QUALITY OF GLAZE, good ; colour, dark blue.

[Davis Collection.]

— **Stopper of a Vase** [47].—Blue glazed faïence.—Height 0 m ·05.—
Maximum diameter 0 m ·045.—Room D.

In the form of an inverted lotus flower, ornamented with four rings round the calyx
painted in black.

QUALITY OF GLAZE, good ; colour, a fine medium blue.

[Davis Collection.]

— **Stopper of a Vase** [48].—Blue glazed faïence.—Height 0 m ·05.—
Maximum diameter 0 m ·045.—Room D.

In the form of an inverted lotus flower, with sepals and petals outlined in black.

QUALITY OF GLAZE, medium ; colour, good medium blue.

The end of the stopper is broken off.

[Davis Collection.]

46316. **Stopper of a Vase** [49].—Blue glazed faïence.—Height 0 m ·035.—
Maximum diameter 0 m ·03.—Room D.

In the form of an inverted lotus flower, without ornamentation.

QUALITY OF GLAZE, bad ; colour, dull blue.

The end of the stopper is broken off.

46317. **Stopper of a Vase** [50].—Blue glazed faïence.—Height 0 m ·045.—
Maximum diameter 0 m ·05.—Room D.

Form similar to No. 46317.

QUALITY OF GLAZE, poor ; colour, dull blue.

Catal. du Musée, n. 46001.   12

— **Stopper of a Vase** [51].—Blue glazed faïence.—Height 0 m ·045.— Maximum diameter 0 m ·05.—-Room D.

Form similar to No. 46317.

QUALITY OF GLAZE, poor; colour, dull blue.

[Davis Collection.]

— **Stopper of a Vase** [52].—Blue glazed faïence.—Height 0 m ·05.— Maximum diameter 0 m ·04.—Room D.

In the form of an inverted lotus flower, with sepals outlined in black, and dotted to represent hairs. Hollow inside.

QUALITY OF GLAZE, medium; colour, medium blue.

[Davis Collection.]

— **Stopper of a Vase** [53].—Blue glazed faïence.—Height 0 m ·05.— Maximum diameter 0 m ·04.—-Room D.

Form and ornamentation similar to No. [52].

QUALITY OF GLAZE, bad; colour, dull blue.

[Davis Collection.]

— **Stopper of a Vase** [54].—Blue glazed faïence.—Height 0 m ·05.— Maximum diameter 0 m ·04.—Room D.

Form and ornamentation similar to No. [52]. Made hollow, and the end of stopper has had papyrus pith twisted round it, and then been stuck into the stopper with wax.

QUALITY OF GLAZE, medium; colour, medium blue.

[Davis Collection.]

— **Stopper of a Vase** [55].—Blue glazed faïence.—Height 0 m ·05.— Maximum diameter 0 m ·04.—Room D.

Form and ornamentation similar to No. [52].

QUALITY OF GLAZE, medium; colour, medium blue.

[Davis Collection.]

— **Stopper of a Vase** [56].—Blue glazed faïence.—Height 0 m ·04.— Maximum diameter 0 m ·035.—Room D.

Form and ornamentation similar to No. [52].

QUALITY OF GLAZE, medium; colour, medium blue.

[Davis Collection.]

— **Stopper of a Vase** [57].—Blue glazed faïence.—Height 0 m ·025.— Diameter 0 m ·055.—Room D.

In the form of three rings of different diameters superimposed upon each other (see figure). With hollow for insertion of the end of the stopper.

QUALITY OF GLAZE, good; colour, good medium blue.

[Davis Collection.]

— **Stopper of a Vase** [58].—Blue glazed faïence.—Height 0 m ·025.— Breadth 0 m ·025.—Room D.

In the form of an inverted lotus flower, with sepals and petals outlined in black.

QUALITY OF GLAZE, good; colour, good medium blue.

[Davis Collection.]

— **Stopper of a Vase** [59].—Blue glazed faïence.—Height 0 m ·025.— Breadth 0 m ·025.—Room D.

Form and ornamentation similar to No. [58].

QUALITY OF GLAZE, good; colour, good medium blue.

[Davis Collection.]

46318. **Stopper of a Vase** [60].—Blue glazed faïence.—Height 0 m ·025.— Breadth 0 m ·025.—Room D.

Form and ornamentation similar to No. [58].

QUALITY OF GLAZE, good; colour, good medium blue.

— **Stopper of a Vase** [61].—Blue glazed faïence.—Height 0 m ·025.— Breadth 0 m ·025.—Room D.

Form and ornamentation similar to No. [58].

QUALITY OF GLAZE, good; colour, good medium blue.

[Davis Collection.]

46319. **Stopper of a Vase** [62].—Blue glazed faïence.—Height 0 m ·025.— Breadth 0 m ·025.—Chamber 3.

Form and ornamentation similar to No. [58].

QUALITY OF GLAZE, good; colour, good medium blue.

16. LIBATION CUPS.

46320.   Libation Cup [1].—Blue glazed faïence.—Height 0 m ·07.—Diameter across mouth 0 m ·09.—Diameter at base 0 m ·055.

In the form of a ▽-shaped cup, with a violet rim.

QUALITY OF GLAZE, medium; colour, medium blue.

Seven pieces (incomplete).

FIG. 42.   FIG. 41.   FIG. 43.

LIBATION CUPS.

—   Libation Cup [2].—Blue glazed faïence.—Height 0 m ·07.—Diameter across mouth 0 m ·07.—Diameter at base 0 m ·045.—See Fig. 41.

In the form for ▽-shaped cup, with a violet rim and four violet lines running round its circumference, two lines near the top and two near the bottom.

QUALITY OF GLAZE, medium; colour, medium blue.

Broken into two pieces (complete).

[Davis Collection.]

46321.   Libation Cup [3].—Blue glazed faïence.—Height 0 m ·065.—Diameter across mouth 0 m ·075.—Diameter at base 0 m ·055.

Shape and ornamentation similar to No. [2].

QUALITY OF GLAZE, medium; colour, medium blue.

Broken into five pieces (complete).

46322.   Libation Cup [4].—Blue glazed faïence.—Height 0 m ·07.—Diameter across mouth 0 m ·077.—Diameter at base 0 m ·053.

In the form of a ▽-shaped cup, with slightly projecting rim and base; ornamentation similar to No. [2].

QUALITY OF GLAZE, medium; colour, medium blue.

Four pieces (incomplete).

46323.   Libation Cup [5].—Blue glazed faïence.—Height 0 m ·085.—Diameter across mouth 0 m ·065.—Diameter at base 0 m ·045.

In form of a ▽-shaped cup, with slightly projecting rim and base.

ORNAMENTATION: rim and base violet; immediately below the rim two parallel violet lines run round the circumference; in the centre two more parallel violet lines, divided on one side by a vertical column, running from the second line of top to upper line of base, containing the following inscription :—

Around the lower part of the cup is a band of violet diamond-shaped lozenges, divided above and below by two parallel violet lines.

QUALITY OF GLAZE, good; colour, lightish blue.

Eight pieces (incomplete).

46324.   Libation Cup [6].—Blue glazed faïence.—Height 0 m ·065.—Diameter across mouth 0 m ·07.—Diameter at base 0 m ·045.—Figure 42.

In the form of a ▽-shaped cup, with violet rim.   Around the cup are three rows of zigzag lines, divided from the rim and base by double violet lines.

QUALITY OF GLAZE, medium; colour, medium blue.

Broken into ten pieces.

46325.   Libation Cup [7].—Blue glazed faïence.—Height 0 m ·06.—Diameter across mouth 0 m ·065.—Diameter at base 0 m ·04.—Figure 43.

In the form of a ▽-shaped cup, with three rows of scale ornament running round its circumference, divided from rim and base by a single horizontal line.

QUALITY OF GLAZE, medium; colour, medium blue.

Five pieces (incomplete).

46326.   Libation Cup [8].—Blue glazed faïence.—Height 0 m ·075.—Diameter across mouth 0 m ·06.—Diameter at base 0 m ·04.

In the form of a ▽-shaped cup, with three sets of double lines running round the circumference, one set near the rim, the second in the centre, and the third near the base.   On a fragment from the lower part of the side occurs the hieroglyph Ⱥ, showing that on the missing side there was one or more vertical columns of hieroglyphs giving the name and titles of Thoutmôsis IV.

QUALITY OF GLAZE, good ; colour, medium blue.

Six pieces (incomplete).

46327.   Libation Cup [9].—Blue glazed faïence.—Height 0 m ·065.—Diameter across mouth 0 m ·065.—Diameter at base 0 m ·042.

In the form of a ▽-shaped cup.

ORNAMENTATION : Immediately below the rim a horizontal violet line, around the cup a row of reeds, alternating with lotus leaves, and near the base a horizontal vertical line, with broad vertical lines connecting it with the base.

QUALITY OF GLAZE, medium ; colour, medium blue.

Five pieces (incomplete).

46328.   Fragment of a Libation Cup [10].—Blue glazed faïence.

In form probably similar to No. [2].   Plain, with violet rim.

PLATE XXIII.

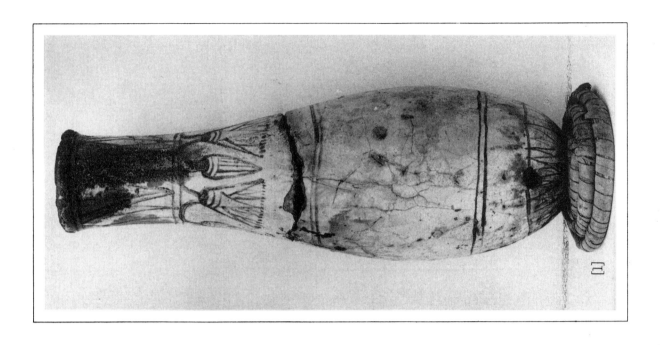

[1]

46347.

VASES.

46329.

17. ⛶-SHAPED VASES.

—   **Vase** [1].—Blue glazed faïence.—Height 0 m ·34.—Maximum diameter 0 m ·105.—Diameter across lip 0 m ·065.—Room D.—Plate XXIII, [1].

⛶-shaped vase, in blue glazed faïence, with ornamentation in black outline.

ORNAMENTATION : *Lip*, violet. *Neck*, a band of inverted lotus petals. *Bowl*, divided into three bands by double lines. In the upper band, hanging from the dividing line, is a row of inverted lotus flowers alternating with buds; interrupting this ornament is the prenomen of Thoutmôsis IV, written vertically and in a cartouche, ⬭⬭. The second band is plain. The lower band, which forms the bottom of the bowl, is plain above, and has a large open lotus flower below.

QUALITY OF GLAZE, very good ; colour, a fine blue.

Broken into four pieces.

[Davis Collection.]

46329.   **Vase** [2].—Blue glazed faïence.—Height 0 m ·34.—Maximum diameter 0 m ·07.—Diameter across lip 0 m ·07.—Room D.—Plate XXIII.

⛶-shaped vase, in blue glazed faïence, with ornamentation in black outline.

ORNAMENTATION : *Lip*, violet. *Neck*, inverted lotus petals. *Bowl*, divided into three bands by rows of rectangles. The upper band is plain, except that on the front is a rectangular panel bearing the following inscription :—

The second band is also plain, save for a double line running round it. The lower band, which forms the bottom of the bowl, is ornamented with a large rosette with drop-like petals.

QUALITY OF GLAZE, fine ; colour, medium blue.

Thirteen pieces (incomplete).

46330.   Vase [3].—Blue glazed faïence.—Maximum diameter 0 m ·115.—Diameter across lip 0 m ·075.—Room D.

⎰-shaped vase, in blue glazed faïence, with ornamentation in black outline.

ORNAMENTATION : *Lip*, plain. *Neck*, a band of inverted lotus petals. *Bowl*, divided into two bands by a double line. The upper band is plain, save for the prenomen of Thoutmôsis IV, which is written vertically on a cartouche in the centre. The lower band, which forms the bottom of the bowl, is ornamented with an open lotus flower.

QUALITY OF GLAZE, fine ; colour, medium blue.

Six pieces (incomplete).

46331.   Vase [4].—Blue glazed faïence.—Height 0 m ·35.—Maximum diameter 0 m ·12.—Diameter across lip 0 m ·07.—Room D.

⎰-shaped vase, in blue glazed faïence, with ornamentation in black outline.

ORNAMENTATION : *Lip*, plain. *Neck*, a band of inverted lotus petals. *Bowl*, divided into three broad bands of about equal size by double lines. The upper two bands are plain ; the lower one, which forms the bottom of the bowl, is ornamented with an open lotus flower.

QUALITY OF GLAZE, fine ; colour, medium blue.

Nine pieces. Remains of ancient mending.

46332.   Fragment of a Vase [5].—Blue glazed faïence.—Maximum diameter 0 m ·115 (?) ; diameter across lip 0 m ·08.—Room D.

Fragment of the neck and part of a ⎯-shaped vase, with ornamentation and inscription similar to No. 46330.

QUALITY OF GLAZE, good ; colour, medium blue.

46333.   Fragment of a Vase [6].—Blue glazed faïence.—Diameter across lip 0 m ·07.—Chamber 3.

Fragment of the neck and bowl of a ⎯-shaped vase, with ornamentation similar to that of No. 46332, except that in the centre of the bowl are the remains of a rectangular panel with the following inscription :

QUALITY OF GLAZE, good ; colour, medium blue.

46334. Fragments of a Vase [7].—Blue glazed faïence.—Diameter across lip 0 m ·07.—Chambers 3 and 4.

Five fragments of the neck and bowl of a ⎕-shaped vase, with ornamentation in black.

ORNAMENTATION. *Neck*, a band of long painted lotus petals. *Bowl*, divided from the neck by a double line, plain, but inscribed on its front with the cartouches of Thoutmôsis IV, surmounted by double feathers : 𓍹⎯𓍺, 𓍹⎯𓍺.

QUALITY OF GLAZE, rough ; colour, medium blue.

Five pieces.

46335. Neck of a Vase [8].—Blue glazed faïence.—Diameter across lip 0 m ·07.—Room D.

Neck of a ⎕-shaped vase, with ornamentation in black.

ORNAMENTATION. *Lip*, dotted, with a black line at the top of the neck. *Neck*, a row of long drop-shaped pendants with a curved line beneath. Separating the neck from the bowl below is a double line, and on the front of the bowl was written vertically, between black lines, the prenomen of Thoutmôsis IV.

QUALITY OF GLAZE, medium ; colour, medium blue.

Four pieces.

46336. Neck of a Vase [9].—Blue glazed faïence.—Diameter across lip 0 m ·075.—Room D.

Neck of a ⎕-shaped vase, with ornamentation in black outline.

ORNAMENTATION : *Neck*, a row of lotus sepals, with double line running round the circumference below. The upper part of the bowl is plain, but bears on it the prenomen of Thoutmôsis IV, in a cartouche, written vertically.

QUALITY OF GLAZE, good ; colour, medium blue.

46337. Fragments of a Vase [10].—Blue glazed faïence.—Diameter across lip 0 m ·08.—Chamber 3.

Fragments of a ⎕-shaped vase, with similar ornamentation to No. 46332.

QUALITY OF GLAZE, good ; colour, medium blue.

Eleven pieces (the whole bottom missing).

46338. Fragments of a Vase [11].—Blue glazed faïence.—Chamber 3.

Five fragments of the neck of a ⎕-shaped vase, with ornamentation in black outline.

ORNAMENTATION : *Neck*, a row of vertical double lines, with, in the spaces between them, (I) zigzag lines arranged ⋀⋀ and (2) plain blue.

QUALITY OF GLAZE, good ; colour, medium blue.

Remains of ancient mending.

Catal. du Musée, n. 46001.

46339.   Fragments of a Vase [12].—Blue glazed faïence.—Diameter across lip 0 m ·07.—Room D.

Six fragments of the neck of a ∏-shaped vase, with ornamentation in black.

ORNAMENTATION: *Neck*, a row of lotus petals in black, divided from the bowl by a double black line.

QUALITY OF GLAZE, inferior (mottled); colour, medium blue.

Remains of ancient mending.

46340.   Vase [13].—Blue glazed faïence.—Height 0 m ·23.—Maximum diameter 0 m ·09.—Chamber 3.

∏-shaped vase, with flat bottom, in blue glazed faïence, with ornamentation in black outline.

ORNAMENTATION: *Neck*, a band of inverted lotus petals in black. *Bowl*, divided into three bands by double lines. The upper band is plain; the second one bears the prenomen of Thoutmôsis IV, written vertically: [hieroglyphs]. The third band, which forms the bottom of the vase, is ornamented with an open lotus flower, having dotted sepals.

QUALITY OF GLAZE, good; colour, medium blue.

The upper rim of the neck is wanting.

46341.   Lower part of a Vase [14].—Blue glazed faïence.—Maximum diameter 0 m ·095.—Chamber 3.

∏-shaped vase, with flat bottom, in blue glazed faïence, with ornamentation in black outline.

ORNAMENTATION: The *bowl* is separated from the neck by a double line, and divided at its greatest diameter by a second double line. The upper band thus formed is plain, save for the prenomen of Thoutmôsis IV, which is written vertically on both sides (back and front): [hieroglyphs]. The lower band, which forms the bottom of the vase, is ornamented with an open lotus flower having dotted sepals.

QUALITY OF GLAZE, very good; colour, light blue.

46342.   Vase [15].—Blue glazed faïence.—Maximum diameter 0 m ·1.— Chamber 3.

∏-shaped vase, with flat bottom, in blue glazed faïence, with ornamentation in black.

ORNAMENTATION: *Neck*, a row of lotus petals in full black. *Bowl*, divided into three bands by double black lines. The uppermost band is plain. In the centre of the second band is, on the front, the prenomen of Thoutmôsis IV, written vertically between double lines. The lower band, which forms the bottom of the bowl, is ornamented with an open lotus flower, having dotted sepals and lined petals.

QUALITY OF GLAZE, good; colour, light blue.

The whole of the rim is missing.

46343.   Vase [16].—Blue glazed faïence.—Maximum diameter 0 m ·09.— Chamber 3.

⋃-shaped vase, with flat bottom, and ornamentation similar to No. 46342, except that the prenomen of Thoutmôsis IV is written vertically in a cartouche, and not between vertical bands : ⌐‡◯ (○ ⊕ ⌐).

QUALITY OF GLAZE, good; colour, light blue.

Six pieces (the whole of the rim is missing).

46344.   Fragment of a Vase [17].—Blue glazed faïence.—Maximum diameter 0 m ·105.—Chamber 3.

Lower part of a ⋂-shaped vase, with ornamentation similar to No. 46340.

QUALITY OF GLAZE, good; colour, medium blue.

46344a. Fragment of a Vase [18].—Blue glazed faïence.—Chamber 3.

Lower part of a ⋂-shaped vase, with ornamentation similar to that of No. 46341.

QUALITY OF GLAZE, good; colour, dark blue.

Three pieces.

46345.   Fragment of a Vase [19].—Blue glazed faïence.—Chamber 3.

Lower part of a ⋃-shaped vase, with ornamentation similar to that of No. 46343.

QUALITY OF GLAZE, good; colour, medium blue.

One piece.

46346.   Vase [20].—Blue glazed faïence.—Height 0 m ·255.—Diameter across lip 0 m ·06.—Maximum diameter 0 m ·105.—Room D.

⋃-shaped vase, without ornamentation.

QUALITY OF GLAZE, medium; colour, medium blue.

Nine pieces (incomplete).

13.

46347.   Vase [21].—Blue glazed faïence.—Height 0 m ·26.—Diameter across lip 0 m ·055.—Maximum diameter 0 m ·10.—Room D.—Plate XXIII.

⎰⎱–shape vase, without ornamentation.

QUALITY OF GLAZE, poor; colour, light blue (much stained).

Fourteen pieces (incomplete).

46348.   Fragments of a Vase [22].—Blue glazed faïence.—Chamber 3.

Fragments of the upper part of a ⎰⎱–shaped vase, without ornamentation.

QUALITY OF GLAZE, fair; colour, light blue.

Four pieces.

46349.   Fragments of a Vase [23].—Blue glazed faïence.—Chamber 4.

Fragments of the upper part of a ⎰⎱–shaped vase, in blue glazed faïence, ornamented by two lines around the upper part of the neck; otherwise plain.

QUALITY OF GLAZE, poor; colour, medium blue.

46350.   Fragments of a Vase [24].—Blue glazed faïence.—Height 0 m ·27.— Diameter across lip 0 m ·08.—Room D.

Fragments of a ⎰⎱–shaped vase, in blue glazed faïence, ornamented by a double line around the upper part of the neck. On the neck is written vertically the prenomen of Thoutmôsis IV in a rectangular panel. Around the lower part of the bowl are two black lines; the bowl is plain.

QUALITY OF GLAZE, medium; colour, medium blue.

Five pieces.

46351.   Neck of a Vase [25].—Blue glazed faïence.—Diameter across lip 0 m ·08.—Room D.

Neck of a ⎰⎱–shaped vase, similar to that of No. 46350, except that above the prenomen of Thoutmôsis IV is written the words ⎾⎿.

QUALITY OF GLAZE, medium; colour, medium blue.

Two pieces.

46352.   Fragments of a Vase [26].—Blue glazed faïence.—Maximum diameter of bowl 0 m ·115.—Diameter across lip 0 m ·065.— Chambers 3 and 4.

Fragments of a ⎰⎱–shaped vase, in blue glazed faïence, with ornamentation in black.

ORNAMENTATION : *Lip*, violet. *Neck*, around the top is a row of lotus sepals, dotted. In the front this row is interrupted by the prenomen of Thoutmôsis IV, written vertically in a cartouche, without base line : (cartouche). *Bowl*, plain.

QUALITY OF GLAZE, medium ; colour, light blue.

Five pieces.

46353. **Fragments of a Vase** [27].—Blue glazed faïence.—Diameter across lip 0 m ·06.—Room D.

Fragments of a ⃞-shaped vase, in blue glazed faïence, with ornamentation in black.

ORNAMENTATION : *Neck*, around the upper part of it are two black lines, and suspended from the lower one a row of lotus petals in full black. In the front this row is interrupted by the prenomen of Thoutmôsis IV, written vertically in a cartouche. *Bowl*, plain.

QUALITY OF GLAZE, medium ; colour, light blue.

Six pieces.

46354. **Fragments of a Vase** [28].—Blue glazed faïence.—Diameter across lip 0 m ·065.—Room D.

Fragments of a ⃞-shaped vase, in blue glazed faïence, with three lines running round the top of the neck, and the prenomen of Thoutmôsis IV written vertically on the front, below.

QUALITY OF GLAZE, medium ; colour, medium blue.

Three pieces.

46355. **Fragments of a Vase** [29].—Blue glazed faïence.—Maximum diameter of bowl 0 m ·115.—Chamber 4 and Room D.

The lower part of a ⃞-shaped vase, with rather more swollen base than any of the preceding. The neck and rim are wanting.

ORNAMENTATION : *Bowl*, around the top of the bowl is a double line dividing it from the base, and from this hangs a row of drop-shaped pendants. Beneath these pendants are two wavy lines, then a narrow plain space. and a large open lotus flower with spreading petals.

QUALITY OF GLAZE, good ; colour, medium blue.

Five pieces.

18. SYMBOLS OF LIFE.

46356. **Symbol of Life** [1].—Blue glazed faïence.—Height 0 m ·245.—Breadth across arms 0 m ·13.—Room D.—Plate XXIV.

The section of the arm and foot is rectangular; that of the hoop, round.

ORNAMENTATION : Obverse and reverse similarly ornamented, with violet-black lines burnt into the blue glaze. One line runs around the centre of the loop, vertical lines cross the arms to near the extremities, where they give place to three horizontal lines. On the foot is the prenomen of Thoutmôsis IV, and beneath it a papyrus flower with long stalk and dotted inflorescence.

QUALITY OF GLAZE, very good ; colour, medium blue.

Broken into seven pieces.

— **Symbol of Life** [2].—Blue glazed faïence.—Height 0 m ·24.—Breadth across arms 0 m ·135.—Room D.

Section and ornamentation similar to No. 46356.

QUALITY OF GLAZE, good ; colour, medium blue.

Broken into five pieces.

[Davis Collection.]

46357. **Symbol of Life** [3].—Blue glazed faïence.—Height 0 m ·225.—Breadth across arms 0 m ·145.—Room D.

Section and ornamentation similar to No. 46356.

QUALITY OF GLAZE, good ; colour, medium blue.

Broken into five pieces.

46358. **Symbol of Life** [4].—Blue glazed faïence.—Height 0 m ·23.—Breadth across arms 0 m ·165.—Room D.

Section and ornamentation similar to No. 46356.

QUALITY OF GLAZE, medium ; colour, varying blue.

Broken into seven pieces.

— **Symbol of Life** [5].—Blue glazed faïence.—Height 0 m ·23.—Breadth across arms 0 m ·13.—Room D.

Section and ornamentation similar to No. 46356.

PLATE XXIV.

[40]

46356.

AMULETS.

QUALITY OF GLAZE, good ; colour, medium blue.

Broken into five pieces.

[Davis Collection.]

46359.   Symbol of Life [6].—Blue glazed faïence.—Height 0 m ·24.—Room D.

Section and ornamentation similar to No. 46356.

QUALITY OF GLAZE, good ; colour, medium blue.

Broken into five pieces ; one arm missing.

46360.   Symbol of Life [7].—Blue glazed faïence.—Height 0 m ·235.—Breadth across arms 0 m ·13.—Room D.

Section and ornamentation similar to No. 46356.

QUALITY OF GLAZE, badly burnt ; colour, a fine rich blue.

Broken into five pieces ; fragment of loop missing.

46361.   Symbol of Life [8].—Blue glazed faïence.—Height 0 m ·23.—Breadth across arms 0 m ·145.—Room D.

Section of arms, foot, and loop rectangular.

ORNAMENTATION : similar to that of No. 46356, but very coarsely executed.

QUALITY OF GLAZE, medium ; colour, medium blue.

Broken into six pieces ; fragment missing from loop.

—   **Symbol of Life** [9].—Blue glazed faïence.—Height 0 m ·23.—Breadth across arms 0 m ·155.—Room D.

Section similar to No. 46361.

ORNAMENTATION : similar to No. 46356, but roughly executed.

QUALITY OF GLAZE, medium ; colour, medium.

Broken into six pieces ; fragment missing from top of loop.

[Davis Collection.]

46362.   Symbol of Life [10].—Blue glazed faïence.—Breadth across arms 0 m ·125.—Room D.

Section similar to No. 46361.

ORNAMENTATION : similar to No. 46356.

QUALITY OF GLAZE, good ; colour, medium.

Broken into five pieces ; two pieces missing from top of loop.

46363. Symbol of Life [11].—Blue glazed faïence.—Breadth across arms
0 m ·135.—Room D.

Section similar to No. 46361.

ORNAMENTATION: similar to No. 46356.

QUALITY OF GLAZE, fair; colour, medium blue.

Broken into four pieces; part of foot and two fragments of loop missing.

46364. Symbol of Life [12].—Blue glazed faïence.—Breadth across arms
0 m ·145.—Room D.

Section of arms, foot, and loop rectangular.

ORNAMENTATION: Obverse and reverse similarly ornamented, with violet-black lines
burnt into the blue glaze. One line runs round the centre of the loop, and is
continued down on both sides to the bottom of the foot. Vertical lines, divided by
horizontal lines above and below, cross the arms to near the extremities, where they
give place to two horizontal lines.

QUALITY OF GLAZE, medium; colour, light blue.

Broken into six pieces; fragments missing from foot and loop.

—   **Symbol of Life** [13].—Blue glazed faïence.—Height 0 m ·28.—
Breadth across arms 0 m ·14.—Room D.

Section and ornamentation similar to No. 46364.

QUALITY OF GLAZE, medium; colour, medium blue.

Broken into seven pieces; fragment missing from side of loop.

[Davis Collection.]

46365. Symbol of Life [14].—Blue glazed faïence.—Height 0 m ·26.—
Breadth across arms 0 m ·14.—Room D.

Section and ornamentation similar to No. 46364.

QUALITY OF GLAZE, medium; colour, medium blue.

Broken into five pieces; much chipped at the top of loop.

46366. Symbol of Life [15].—Blue glazed faïence.—Height 0 m ·275.—
Breadth across arms 0 m ·145.—Room D.

Section of arms, loop, and foot rectangular.

ORNAMENTATION: Obverse and reverse similarly ornamented, with violet-black lines
burnt into the blue glaze. One line runs round the centre of the loop, and is
continued down the centre of the foot. Two horizontal lines are drawn on either
side of a number of vertical lines across the two arms to near their extremities,
where they give place to two horizontal lines.

QUALITY OF GLAZE, medium ; colour, medium blue.

Broken into six pieces; side of loop missing.

— **Symbol of Life** [16].—Blue glazed faïence.—Height 0 m ·275.—
Breadth across arms 0 m ·145.—Room D.

Section and ornamentation similar to No. 46366.

QUALITY OF GLAZE, poor ; colour, medium blue.

Broken into five pieces; top of loop missing.

[Davis Collection.]

46367. Symbol of Life [17].—Blue glazed faïence.—Breadth across arms
0 m ·12.—Room D.

Section and ornamentation similar to No. 46366.

QUALITY OF GLAZE, medium; colour, medium blue.

Broken into five pieces; top of loop missing.

46368. Symbol of Life [18].—Blue glazed faïence.—Height 0 m ·23.—
Breadth across arms 0 m ·12.—Room D.

Section of arms, loop, and foot rectangular.

ORNAMENTATION : Obverse and reverse similarly ornamented, with violet-black lines
burnt into the blue glaze. One line runs round the centre of the loop. The arms
are outlined by two horizontal lines, the centre part being crossed by a series of
vertical lines, their extremities being shaped and ornamented like a lotus flower.
Three vertical lines run along the foot, the centre one dividing into two near
the top.

QUALITY OF GLAZE, good ; colour, medium blue.

Broken into six pieces.

46369. Symbol of Life [19].—Blue glazed faïence.—Height 0 m ·225.—
Breadth across arms 0 m ·115.—Room D.

Section and ornamentation similar to No. 46368.

QUALITY OF GLAZE, very fine ; colour, medium blue.

Broken into five pieces.

46370. Symbol of Life [20].—Blue glazed faïence.—Height 0 m ·23.—
Breadth across arms 0 m ·115.—Room D.

Section and ornamentation similar to No. 46368.

QUALITY OF GLAZE, fine ; colour, medium blue.

Broken into five pieces, with marks of ten drying pellets on the glaze.

46371. Symbol of Life [21].—Blue glazed faïence.—Room D.

Section and ornamentation similar to No. 46368.

QUALITY OF GLAZE, irregular and badly burnt; colour, medium blue.

Broken into three pieces; one arm and greater part of loop wanting.

46372. Symbol of Life [22].—Blue glazed faïence.—Breadth across arms
0 m ·11.—Room D.

Section and ornamentation similar to No. 46368.

QUALITY OF GLAZE, fair; colour, medium blue.

Two fragments only.

46373. Symbol of Life [23].—Blue glazed faïence.—Height 0 m ·21.—
Breadth across arms 0 m ·11.—Room D.

Section of arms, loop and foot rectangular.

ORNAMENTATION: Obverse and reverse ornamented with violet-black lines burnt into
the blue glaze. *Obverse:* One line runs round the centre of the loop: the arms are
crossed by vertical lines to near the centre, where they give place to the prenomen
of Thoutmôsis IV. A central line runs down the foot. *Reverse:* Similar to obverse,
but without the prenomen of Thoutmôsis IV.

QUALITY OF GLAZE, fine; colour, medium blue.

Broken into three pieces, with marks of drying pellets on the glaze.

46374. Symbol of Life [24].—Blue glazed faïence.—Height 0 m ·215.—
Breadth across arms 0 m ·11.—Room D.

Section and ornamentation similar to No. [23].

QUALITY OF GLAZE, fair; colour, medium blue.

Broken into five pieces.

46375. Symbol of Life [25].—Blue glazed faïence.—Height 0 m ·2.—
Breadth across arms 0 m ·105.—Room D.

Section and ornamentation similar to No. [23].

QUALITY OF GLAZE, good; colour, medium blue.

Broken into three pieces.

46376. Symbol of Life [26].—Blue glazed faïence.—Height 0 m ·20.— Room D.

Section and ornamentation similar to No. [23].

QUALITY OF GLAZE, good; colour, fine blue.

Broken into three pieces; arm and part of loop missing.

46377. Symbol of Life [27].—Blue glazed faïence.—Height 0 m ·25.— Breadth across arms 0 m ·15.—Room D.

Section of arms, loop and foot rectangular.

ORNAMENTATION: Obverse and reverse ornamented by violet-black lines burnt into the blue glaze. *Obverse:* One line runs round the centre of the loop. The arms are outlined by a horizontal line running round them, the centre part being crossed by vertical lines, the extremities by five horizontal lines. The foot is outlined by a line running down the sides and across the base, and halfway up the foot is the prenomen of Thoutmôsis IV. *Reverse:* Similar to obverse, but in place of the cartouche is a single vertical line running from the arms to the base.

QUALITY OF GLAZE, bad and meagre; colour, greeny-blue.

Broken into six pieces.

46378. Symbol of Life [28].—Blue glazed faïence.—Height 0 m ·26.— Breadth across arms 0 m ·15.—Room D.

Section similar to No. 46377.

ORNAMENTATION: Similar to No. 46377, but with no central line on foot of reverse.

QUALITY OF GLAZE, bad and meagre; colour, greeny-blue.

Broken into five pieces.

46378a. Symbol of Life [29].—Blue glazed faïence.—Height 0 m ·27.— Breadth across arms 0 m ·16.—Room D.

Section and ornamentation similar to No. 46377.

QUALITY OF GLAZE, good; colour, light blue.

Broken into five pieces, foot missing.

46379. Symbol of Life [30].—Blue glazed faïence.—Height 0 m ·22.— Breadth across arms 0 m 12.—Room D.

Section of arms, foot and loop rectangular; a circular hole in the upper part of the loop.

ORNAMENTATION: Obverse and reverse ornamented by violet-black lines burnt into the blue glaze. *Obverse:* One line runs round the centre of the hoop. Between

14.

the two arms is the prenomen of Thoutmôsis IV. The arms are crossed by vertical lines outlined on both sides by a horizontal line, except near the edges, where there are six vertical lines. On the foot a line runs right round with a vertical line in the centre dividing near the base into two. *Reverse:* The only ornamentation is a single line running round the loop.

QUALITY OF GLAZE, good; colour, medium blue.

Broken into five pieces.

— **Symbol of Life** [31].—Blue glazed faïence.—Height 0 m ·22.— Breadth across arms 0 m ·13.—Room D.

Section of arms, foot rectangular, loop round.

ORNAMENTATION: Obverse and reverse ornamented by violet-black lines burnt into the blue glaze. *Obverse:* Similar to No. 46379, but with a double line ending in a lotus flower running down the centre of the foot. *Reverse:* No ornamentation.

QUALITY OF GLAZE, good; colour, medium blue.

Broken into five pieces; part of loop missing.

[Davis Collection.]

46380-7. Fragments of eight Symbols of Life [32–39].—Belonging to various types.

— **Symbol of Life** [40].—Blue glazed faïence.—Height 0 m ·15.— Breadth across arms 0 m ·07.—Room D.—Plate XXIV [40].

Symbol of Life, in blue glazed faïence, roughly modelled, and ornamented with black lines. The centre part is solid, and at the top is a circular plate.

QUALITY OF GLAZE, fair; colour, medium blue.

Broken into two pieces (complete).

[Davis Collection.]

46388. Symbol of Life [41].—Blue glazed faïence.—Height 0 m ·17.— Room D.

Symbol of Life, similar to No. [40].

QUALITY OF GLAZE, medium; colour, medium blue.

Two pieces (part of one arm missing).

46389. Symbol of Life [42].—Blue glazed faïence.—Height 0 m ·145 (?).— Breadth across arms 0 m ·07.—Room D.

Symbol of Life, similar to No. [40].

QUALITY OF GLAZE, medium; colour, medium blue.

Two pieces (top missing).

46390. Symbol of Life [43].—Blue glazed faïence.—Height 0 m ·15 (?).—Breadth across arms 0 m ·07.—Room D.

Symbol of Life, similar to No. [40], but inscribed with the prenomen of Thoutmôsis IV, written in black in the centre of the oval loop.

QUALITY OF GLAZE, medium ; colour, medium blue.

Two pieces (top missing).

46391. Symbol of Life [44].—Blue glazed faïence.—Height 0 m ·15 (?).—Breadth across arms 0 m ·075.—Room D.

Symbol of Life, similar to No. [40], but inscribed with the prenomen of Thoutmôsis IV, written in black in the centre of the oval loop on one side, and his nomen in the centre of the other side.

QUALITY OF GLAZE, medium ; colour, medium blue.

One piece (top missing).

46392. Symbol of Life [45].—Blue glazed faïence.—Breadth across arms 0 m ·07.—Room D.

Symbol of Life, similar to No. [40], but without ornamentation.

QUALITY OF GLAZE, poor ; colour, medium blue.

Two pieces (top wanting).

46393. Symbol of Life [46].—Blue glazed faïence.—Height 0 m ·15.—Breadth across arms 0 m ·07.—Room D.

Symbol of Life, similar to No. 46390.

QUALITY OF GLAZE, medium ; colour, medium blue.

Two pieces (top wanting).

46394-7. Fragments of Symbols of Life [47–50].—Blue glazed faïence.—Room D.

Fragments of four symbols of life similar to No. 46390.

46398-403. Fragments of Symbols of Life [51–56].—Blue glazed faïence.—Room D.

Fragments of the upper parts of five symbols of life, with a narrow bar above No. 46398 bears traces of ancient mending.

19. MODEL THROW-STICKS.

46404. Model Throw-stick [1].—Blue glazed faïence.—Length 0 m ·48.—
Room D.—Plate XXV.

Model throw-stick, in blue glazed faïence, ornamented in black outline on both sides
with the following designs in successive bands : (1) Tip, a conventional lotus flower,
with recurved sepals, from which hang drops of water ; (2) an inverted lotus flower,
with sharply-pointed sepals, dotted to represent hairs ; (3 and 5) the sacred eyes
, with between them (4) the prenomen of Thoutmôsis IV,
(6 to 9) plain ; (10) a lotus flower, similar to that of band (2).

QUALITY OF GLAZE, very fine ; colour, a superb dark blue.

Broken into four pieces (complete).

—   Model Throw-stick [2].—Blue glazed faïence.—Length 0 m ·485.—
Room D.

Model throw-stick, in blue glazed faïence, with ornamentation similar to that of
No. 46404.

QUALITY OF GLAZE, very fine ; colour, a fine dark blue.

Broken into five pieces (complete).

[Davis Collection.]

46405. Model Throw-stick [3].—Blue glazed faïence.—Length 0 m ·48.—
Room D.

Model throw-stick, in blue glazed faïence, with ornamentation similar to that of
No. 46404, but with the prenomen of Thoutmôsis IV on the upper surface, and
nomen on the under side.

QUALITY OF GLAZE, good, but chipped ; colour, dark blue.

Broken into seven pieces (complete).

46406. Model Throw-stick [4].—Blue glazed faïence.—Length 0 m ·33.—
Room D.—Plate XXV.

Model throw-stick, in blue glazed faïence, ornamented in black outline on both sides
with the following designs in successive bands : (1) Tip, an inverted lotus flower,
with pointed petals and sepals, dotted to represent hairs ; (2) a sacred eye ; (3) the
prenomen of Thoutmôsis IV, enclosed in a double-lined rectangle and written
vertically ; (4) plain ; (5) a lotus flower with lined (representing ribbed) sepals.

PLATE XXV.

46404.   46409.   46406.

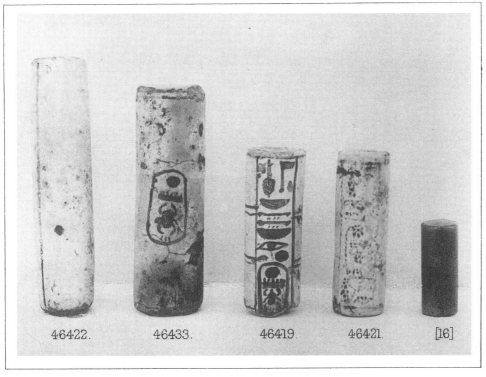

46422.   46433.   46419.   46421.   [16]

MODEL THROWSTICKS & PAPYRUS ROLLS.

QUALITY OF GLAZE, good ; colour, dark blue.

Broken into five pieces (complete).

— **Model Throw-stick** [5].—Blue glazed faïence.—Length 0 m ·33.— Room D.

Model throw-stick, with ornamentation similar to that of No. 46406.

QUALITY OF GLAZE, good ; colour, dark blue.

Broken into three pieces (complete).

[Davis Collection.]

46407. Model Throw-stick [6].—Blue glazed faïence.—Length 0 m ·33.— Room D.

Model throw-stick, with ornamentation similar to that of No. 46406.

QUALITY OF GLAZE, good ; colour, dark blue.

Four pieces (incomplete).

46408. Model Throw-stick [7].—Blue glazed faïence.—Length 0 m ·33.— Room D.

Model throw-stick, with ornamentation similar to that of No. 46406, except that the names of the king are enclosed in cartouches.

QUALITY OF GLAZE good ; colour, dark blue.

Three pieces (incomplete).

46409. Model Throw-stick [8].—Blue glazed faïence.—Length 0 m ·27.— Room D.—Plate XXV.

Model throw-stick, in blue glazed faïence, with the following ornamentation in black outline on the upper surface in successive bands : (1) Tip, a conventional lotus flower with recurved sepals ; (2) the sacred eye drawn *across* the bend ; (3) the nomen of Thoutmôsis ; (4) a lotus flower with pointed petals. The under side is only ornamented at the two ends.

QUALITY OF GLAZE, very good ; colour, light blue.

Broken into four pieces (complete).

46410. Model Throw-stick [9].—Blue glazed faïence.—Length 0 m ·27.— Room D.

Model throw-stick, with ornamentation similar to that of No. 46409.

QUALITY OF GLAZE, good ; colour, light blue.

Broken into three pieces (complete).

—   **Model Throw-stick** [10].—Blue glazed faïence.—Length 0 m ·27.—
Room D.

Model throw-stick, with ornamentation similar to that of No. 46409.

QUALITY OF GLAZE, good ; colour, light blue.

Broken into five pieces (complete).

[Davis Collection.]

46411.   Model Throw-stick [11].—Blue glazed faïence.—Length 0 m ·25.—
Room D.

Model throw-stick, in blue glazed faïence, with the following ornamentation in black
outline on the upper and lower surface in successive bands, divided by double
black lines : (1) Tip, a conventional lotus flower with recurved sepals and long
stalk ; (2 and 3) Two sacred eyes 𓂀𓂀 ; (4 and 5) plain ; (6) a lotus flower, with
pointed sepals and petals.

QUALITY OF GLAZE, very good ; colour, light blue.

Four pieces (piece wanting for centre).

46412.   Model Throw-stick [12].—Blue glazed faïence.—Length 0 m ·355.—
Room D.

Model throw-stick, with ornamentation similar to that of No. 46411.

QUALITY OF GLAZE, good ; colour, light blue.

Broken into five pieces (complete).

46413.   Model Throw-stick [13].—Blue glazed faïence.—Length 0 m ·335.—
Room D.

Model throw-stick, with ornamentation similar to that of No. 46411.

QUALITY OF GLAZE, good ; colour; light blue.

Broken into four pieces (complete).

46414.   Model Throw-stick [14].—Blue glazed faïence.—Length 0 m ·30.—
Room D.

Model throw-stick, with ornamentation similar to that of No. 46411, but with the
prenomen of Thoutmôsis IV written in a cartouche between the sacred eyes.

QUALITY OF GLAZE, good ; colour, light blue.

Broken into four pieces (complete).

46415. Model Throw-stick [15].—Blue glazed faïence.—Length 0 m ·30.— Room D.

Model throw-stick, with ornamentation similar to that of No. 46411.

QUALITY OF GLAZE, good ; colour, light blue.

Five pieces (incomplete).

— **Model Throw-stick** [16].—Blue glazed faïence.—Length 0 m ·33.— Room D.

Model throw-stick, in blue glazed faïence, with the following ornamentation in black outline on the upper and lower surface, in successive bands, divided by double black lines : (1) Tip, a conventional lotus flower, with two curved and two recurved sepals ; (2 and 4) the two sacred eyes facing right and left, with between them (3) the prenomen of Thoutmôsis IV written across the blade ; (5 and 6) plain ; (7) at the end is an open lotus flower with dotted sepals.

QUALITY OF GLAZE, good ; colour, medium blue.

Three pieces (complete).

[Davis Collection.]

46416. Model Throw-stick [17].—Blue glazed faïence.—Length 0 m ·34.— Room D.

Model throw-stick, with ornamentation similar to that of No. [16].

QUALITY OF GLAZE, good ; colour, medium blue.

Broken into five pieces (complete).

46417. Model Throw-stick [18].—Blue glazed faïence.—Length 0 m ·34.— Room D.

Model throw-stick, with ornamentation similar to that of No. [16].

QUALITY OF GLAZE, good ; colour, medium blue.

Broken into four pieces (complete).

46418. Model Throw-stick [19].—Blue glazed faïence.—Length 0 m ·34.— Room D.

Model throw-stick, with ornamentation similar to that of No. [16].

QUALITY OF GLAZE, good ; colour, medium blue.

Two pieces (incomplete).

20. MODEL PAPYRUS ROLLS.

46419. Model Papyrus Roll [1].—Blue glazed faïence.—Length 0 m ·09.— Diameter 0 m ·03¼.—Room D.—Plate XXV.

Model of a cylindrical-shaped papyrus roll, in blue glazed faïence. The papyrus is represented rolled tightly up and tied by four bands of string, the latter being shown by double black lines. On the two ends the coils of the papyrus are shown by black coiled lines. Down the front of the roll is a vertical column of hieroglyphs reading: ⌇⌇⌇⌇⌇⌇⌇⌇⌇.

Quality of Glaze, very good; colour, dark blue.

Slightly chipped at the edges.

46420. Model Papyrus Roll [2].—Blue glazed faïence.—Length 0 m ·09.— Diameter 0 m ·03¼.—Room D.

Model of a cylindrical-shaped papyrus roll, similar to No. 1, except that the inscription gives the nomen of Thoutmôsis IV as follows: ⌇⌇⌇⌇⌇⌇⌇⌇ *sic.*

Quality of Glaze, very good; colour, dark blue.

—   **Model Papyrus Roll** [3].—Blue glazed faïence.—Length 0 m ·09.— Diameter 0 m ·03.

Model of a cylindrical-shaped papyrus roll, similar to No. 46421, but with inscription as follows: ⌇⌇⌇⌇⌇⌇⌇⌇ *sic.*

Quality of Glaze, very good; colour, dark blue.

[Davis Collection.]

46421. Model Papyrus Roll [4].—Blue glazed faïence.—Length 0 m ·09.— Diameter 0 m ·03.—Room D.—Plate XXV.

Model of a cylindrical-shaped papyrus roll, similar to No. 1, but with inscription as follows: ⌇⌇⌇⌇⌇⌇⌇⌇ *sic.*

Quality of Glaze, poor; colour, dark blue.

— **Model Papyrus Roll** [5].—Blue glazed faïence.—Length 0 m ·09.—Diameter 0 m ·03.

Model of a cylindrical-shaped papyrus roll, similar to No. 1, but with inscription as follows: 𓏤𓈖𓍳𓍹𓏤𓆣𓏤𓏥𓍺𓂝𓃀𓏥 .

QUALITY OF GLAZE, poor; colour, dark blue.

[Davis Collection.]

46422. **Model Papyrus Roll** [6].—Blue glazed faïence.—Length 0 m ·14.—Diameter 0 m ·03.—Room D.—Plate XXV.

Model of a cylindrical papyrus roll, ornamented by a vertical black line running across one side from end to end, and coils in black on the two ends.

QUALITY OF GLAZE, good; colour, very pale blue.

— **Model Papyrus Roll** [7].—Blue glazed faïence.—Length 0 m ·14.—Diameter 0 m ·03.—Chamber 3.

Model of a cylindrical papyrus roll, similar to No. 46424.

QUALITY OF GLAZE, good; colour, very pale blue.

Broken into two pieces (complete).

[Davis Collection.]

— **Model Papyrus Roll** [8].—Blue glazed faïence.—Length 0 m ·14.—Diameter 0 m ·03.—Room D.

Model of a cylindrical papyrus roll, similar to No. 46424.

QUALITY OF GLAZE, good; colour, very pale blue.

Broken into two pieces (complete).

[Davis Collection.]

46423. **Model Papyrus Roll** [9].—Blue glazed faïence.—Length 0 m ·14.—Diameter 0 m ·03.—Room D.

Model of a cylindrical papyrus roll, similar to No. 46422.

QUALITY OF GLAZE, good; colour, very pale blue.

Broken into two pieces (complete).

46424. **Model Papyrus Roll** [10].—Blue glazed faïence.—Length 0 m ·14.—Diameter 0 m ·03.—Room D.

Model of a cylindrical papyrus roll, similar to No. 46422.

QUALITY OF GLAZE, good; colour, very pale blue.

Broken into two pieces (complete).

46425. Model Papyrus Roll [11].—Blue glazed faïence.—Length 0 m ·14.—Diameter 0 m ·03.—Room D.

Model of a cylindrical papyrus roll, similar to No. 46422.

QUALITY OF GLAZE, good; colour, very pale blue.

Broken into two pieces (complete).

46426. Model Papyrus Roll [12].—Blue glazed faïence.—Length 0 m ·14.—Diameter 0 m ·03.—Room D.

Model of a cylindrical papyrus roll, similar to No. 46422.

QUALITY OF GLAZE, good; colour, very pale blue.

Broken into two pieces (complete).

46427. Model Papyrus Roll [13].—Blue glazed faïence.—Length 0 m ·14.—Diameter 0 m ·03.—Room D.

Model of a cylindrical papyrus roll, similar to No. 46422.

QUALITY OF GLAZE, good; colour, very pale blue.

Broken into two pieces (complete).

46428. Model Papyrus Roll [14].—Blue glazed faïence.—Length 0 m ·14.—Diameter 0 m ·03.—Room D.

Model of a cylindrical papyrus roll, similar to No. 46422.

QUALITY OF GLAZE, good; colour, very pale blue.

Two pieces (incomplete).

46429. Model Papyrus Roll [15].—Blue glazed faïence.—Length 0 m ·14.—Diameter 0 m ·03.—Room D.

Model of a cylindrical papyrus roll, similar to No. 46422.

QUALITY OF GLAZE, fair; colour, very pale blue.

Broken into six pieces (incomplete).

—   **Model Papyrus Roll** [16].—Blue glazed faïence.—Length 0 m ·05.—Diameter 0 m ·02.—Room D.—Plate XXV [16].

Model of a cylindrical papyrus roll, with a modelled indentation down centre and painted coil at either end.

QUALITY OF GLAZE, superb; colour, very rich dark blue.

[Davis Collection.]

— **Model Papyrus Roll** [17].—Blue glazed faïence.—Length 0 m ·05.—Diameter 0 m ·02.—Room **D**.

Model of a cylindrical papyrus roll, similar to No. [16].

QUALITY OF GLAZE, very fine; colour, very rich dark blue.

[Davis Collection.]

46430. **Model Papyrus Roll** [18].—Blue glazed faïence.—Length 0 m ·05.—Diameter 0 m ·015.—Room **D**.

Model of a cylindrical papyrus roll, with a modelled indentation down centre and modelled coil at either end.

QUALITY OF GLAZE, very fine; colour, rich dark blue.

46431. **Model Papyrus Roll** [19].—Blue glazed faïence.—Length 0 m ·05.—Diameter 0 m ·015.—Room **D**.

Model of a cylindrical papyrus roll, similar to No. [16].

QUALITY OF GLAZE, very fine; colour, rich dark blue.

46432. **Model Papyrus Roll** [20].—Blue glazed faïence.—Length 0 m ·045.—Diameter 0 m ·01.—Room **D**.

Model of a cylindrical papyrus roll, similar to No. [16].

QUALITY OF GLAZE, very fine; colour, rich dark blue.

46433. **Cylinder** [21].—Blue glazed faïence.—Length 0 m ·12.—Diameter 0 m ·04.—Room **D**.—Plate **XXV**.

Cylinder, in blue glazed faïence, ornamented with a black line running around the circumference at either end and the prenomen of Thoutmôsis IV written in a vertical line on the centre: .

QUALITY OF GLAZE, good; colour, medium blue.

Complete.

— **Cylinder** [22].—Blue glazed faïence.—Length 0 m ·12.—Diameter 0 m ·04.—Room **D**.

Cylinder, in blue glazed faïence, similar to No. 46433.

QUALITY OF GLAZE, good; colour, medium blue.

Broken into two pieces (complete).

[Davis Collection.]

46434.   Cylinder [23].—Blue glazed faïence.—Length 0 m ·12.—Diameter 0 m ·04.—Room D.

Cylinder, in blue glazed faïence, similar to No. 46433.

QUALITY OF GLAZE, good; colour, medium blue.

Broken into three pieces (complete).

46435.   Cylinder [24].—Blue glazed faïence.—Length 0 m ·12.—Diameter 0 m ·04.—Room D.

Cylinder, in blue glazed faïence, similar to No. 46433.

QUALITY OF GLAZE, good; colour, medium blue.

Broken into two pieces (a small fragment missing).

46436.   Fragment of a Cylinder [25].—Blue glazed faïence.—Length 0 m ·06.—Diameter 0 m ·04.—Room D.

Fragment of a cylinder, in blue glazed faïence, similar to No. 46433.

QUALITY OF GLAZE, good; colour, medium blue.

—   **Cylinder** [26].—Blue glazed faïence.—Length 0 m ·12.—Diameter 0 m ·04.—Room D.

Cylinder, in blue glazed faïence, similar to No. 46433.

QUALITY OF GLAZE, good; colour, medium blue.

Complete.

[Davis Collection.]

21. BRACELETS.

46437.   Bracelet [1].—Blue glazed faïence.—Diameter 0 m ·10.—Breadth 0 m ·015.—Depth 0 m ·01.

Bracelet, of blue glazed faïence, in the form of a plain ring of rectangular section.

QUALITY OF GLAZE, good; colour, brilliant medium blue.

Broken into six pieces (complete).

46438.   Bracelet [2].—Blue glazed faïence.—Diameter 0 m ·09.—Breadth 0 m ·01.—Depth 0 m ·005.

Bracelet, of blue glazed faïence, in the form of a plain ring of rectangular section.

QUALITY OF GLAZE, medium; colour, medium blue.

Broken into five pieces (complete).

46439.   Bracelet [3].—Blue glazed faïence.—Diameter 0 m ·1.—Breadth 0 m ·015.—Depth 0 m ·01.

Bracelet, of blue glazed faïence, in the form of a plain ring of rectangular section.

QUALITY OF GLAZE, good; colour, medium blue.

Broken into six pieces (complete).

46440.   Bracelet [4].—Blue glazed faïence.—Diameter 0 m ·1.—Breadth 0 m ·015.—Depth 0 m ·01.

Bracelet, of blue glazed faïence, in the form of a plain ring of rectangular section.

QUALITY OF GLAZE, medium (roughish); colour, medium blue.

Broken into six pieces.

46441.   Bracelet [5].—Blue glazed faïence.—Diameter 0 m ·1.—Breadth 0 m ·017.—Depth 0 m ·007.

Bracelet, of blue glazed faïence, in the form of a plain ring of rectangular section.

QUALITY OF GLAZE, very fine; colour, brilliant medium blue.

Broken into four pieces (incomplete).

46442.   **Bracelet** [6].—Blue glazed faïence.—Diameter 0 m ·1.—Breadth 0 m ·015.—Depth 0 m ·005.

Bracelet, of blue glazed faïence, in the form of a ring of rectangular section.

QUALITY OF GLAZE, very good; colour, brilliant medium blue.

Broken into seven pieces (incomplete).

46443.   **Bracelet** [7].—Blue glazed faïence.—Diameter 0 m ·1.—Breadth 0 m ·015.—Depth 0 m ·01.

Bracelet, of blue glazed faïence, in the form of a plain ring of rectangular section.

QUALITY OF GLAZE, very good; colour, brilliant medium blue.

Broken into five pieces (incomplete).

46444.   **Bracelet** [8].—Blue glazed faïence.—Diameter 0 m ·1.—Breadth 0 m ·015.—Depth 0 m ·01.

Bracelet, of blue glazed faïence, in the form of a plain ring of rectangular section.

QUALITY OF GLAZE, medium; colour, medium blue.

Broken into four pieces (incomplete).

46445.   **Bracelet** [9].—Blue glazed faïence.—Diameter 0 m ·1.—Breadth 0 m ·016.—Depth 0 m ·01.

Bracelet, of blue glazed faïence, in the form of a plain ring of rectangular section.

QUALITY OF GLAZE, medium (roughish); colour, medium blue.

Broken into five pieces (incomplete).

46446.   **Bracelet** [10].—Blue glazed faïence.—Diameter 0 m ·085.—Breadth 0 m ·016.—Depth 0 m ·005.

Bracelet, of blue glazed faïence, in the form of a plain ring of rectangular section.

QUALITY OF GLAZE, very good; colour medium blue.

Broken into six pieces (incomplete).

46447.   **Bracelet** [11].—Blue glazed faïence.—Diameter 0 m ·09.—Breadth 0 m ·02.—Depth 0 m ·05.

Bracelet, of blue glazed faïence, in the form of a ring of rectangular section.

QUALITY OF GLAZE, very good; colour, medium blue.

Five pieces (incomplete).

46448. **Bracelet** [12].—Blue glazed faïence.—Diameter 0 m ·1.—Breadth 0 m ·013.—Depth 0 m ·01.

Bracelet, of blue glazed faïence, in the form of a ring of rectangular section.

QUALITY OF GLAZE, medium; colour, medium blue.

Five pieces (incomplete).

46449. **Bracelet** [13].—Blue glazed faïence.—Diameter 0 m ·1.—Breadth 0 m ·015.—Depth 0 m ·01.

Bracelet, of blue glazed faïence, in the form of a ring of rectangular section.

QUALITY OF GLAZE, medium (roughish); colour, medium blue.

Three pieces (incomplete).

46450. **Bracelet** [14].—Blue glazed faïence.—Diameter 0 m ·1.—Breadth 0 m ·017.—Depth 0 m ·05.

Bracelet, of blue glazed faïence, in the form of a ring of rectangular section.

QUALITY OF GLAZE, good; colour, medium blue.

[Seventy-five fragments of bracelets, of blue glazed faïence, in the form of rings of rectangular section and similar to the above.]

22. PLAQUES AND BOXES.

— **Plaque** [1].—Faïence, glazed.—Length 0 m ·125.—Width 0 m ·087.—
Depth 0 m ·008.—Chamber 3.—Plate XXVI [1].

Rectangular plaque, with a narrow circular hole at the lower end.

ORNAMENTATION: Near the centre of the lower half is written in violet a cartouche
containing the prenomen of Thoutmôsis IV enclosed in a rectangle. Around the
edge of the upper surface of the plaque is a narrow band of violet.

QUALITY OF GLAZE, medium; colour, light blue.

Broken into six pieces (nearly complete).

[Davis Collection.]

46451. **Plaque** [2].—Faïence, glazed.—Length 0 m ·12.—Width 0 m ·08.—
Depth 0 m ·008.—Chamber 3.

Rectangular plaque, with a narrow circular hole at the lower end.

ORNAMENTATION: similar to No. [1].

QUALITY OF GLAZE, medium; colour, light blue.

Broken into ten pieces (nearly complete).

46452. **Box** [3].—Faïence, glazed.—Length 0 m ·06.—Width 0 m ·041.—
Height 0 m ·042.—Chamber 3.

Plain rectangular box, with movable lid pierced by narrow holes at both ends.

QUALITY OF GLAZE, good; colour, bright blue.

Both ends of the box are missing.

46453. **Lid of a Box** [4].—Faïence, glazed.—Length 0 m ·077.—Width
0 m ·042.—Chamber 3.

Lid of a box, rectangular in shape and pierced with a hole at one end. The edges are
grooved on the underside. Down the centre of the lid is a vertical line of incised
hieroglyphs reading: ⌷⌷⌷ with a vertical incised line on either side.

QUALITY OF GLAZE, good; colour, a fine medium blue.

Broken into five pieces.

PLATE XXVI.

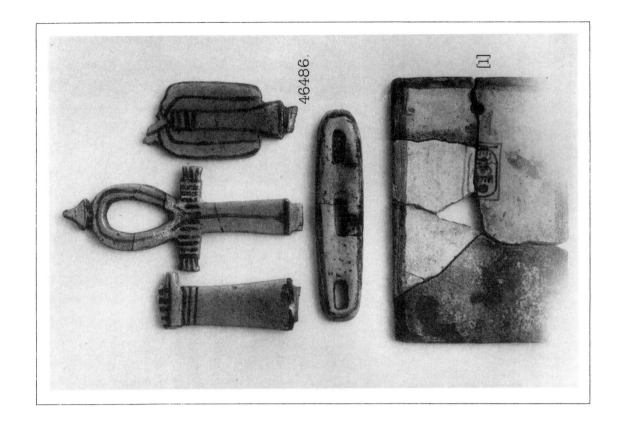

46486.

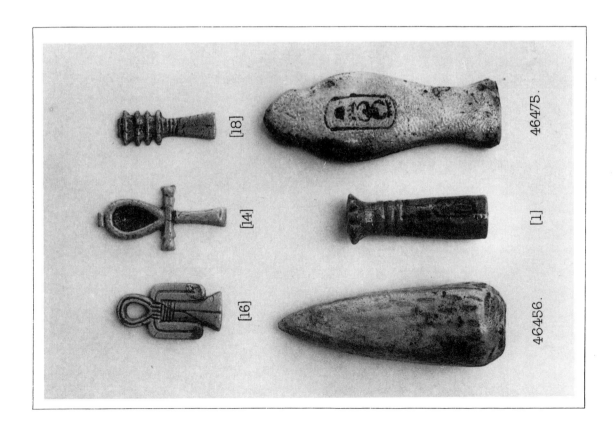

AMULETS.

46454. **Fragments of a Box** [5].—Blue glazed faïence.—Length 0 m ·083.—Width 0 m ·05.—Depth 0 m ·043.—Room **D.**

Eight fragments of a plain rectangular box, in blue glazed faïence: the lid and part of one end wanting.   There is a small hole at either end for inserting a wooden peg to tie the lid on.

QUALITY OF GLAZE, good; colour, medium blue.

46455. **Fragments of Plaques** [6].—Blue glazed faïence.—Found in débris outside tomb.

Two fragments of blue glazed faïence plaques, with parts of human figures modelled in low relief on the upper surface.

QUALITY OF GLAZE, good; colour, lightish blue.

23. MODEL LOTUS BUDS.

46456. **Model Lotus Bud** [1].—Blue glazed faïence.—Height 0 m ·11.—
Maximum diameter 0 m ·038.—Room Y.—Plate XXVI.

Model lotus bud, with sepals outlined in black and hairs represented by short
black lines.

QUALITY OF GLAZE, fine; colour, medium blue.

—   **Model Lotus Bud** [2].—Blue glazed faïence.—Height 0 m ·105.—
Maximum diameter 0 m ·04.—Room Y.

Model lotus bud, with ornamentation similar to No. 46456.

QUALITY OF GLAZE, very fine; colour, a medium brilliant blue.

[Davis Collection.]

46457. **Model Lotus Bud** [3].—Blue glazed faïence.—Height 0 m ·105.—
Maximum diameter 0 m ·035.—Room Y.

Model lotus bud, with ornamentation similar to No. 46456.

QUALITY OF GLAZE, good; colour, medium blue.

Tip of bud broken.

46458. **Model Lotus Bud** [4].—Blue glazed faïence.—Height 0 m ·085.—
Maximum diameter 0 m ·04.—Room R.

Model lotus bud, ornamented with vertical and zigzag lines painted in black.

QUALITY OF GLAZE, fine; colour, medium blue.

Tip of bud broken.

46459. **Model Lotus Bud** [5].—Blue glazed faïence.—Height 0 m ·09.—
Maximum diameter 0 m ·04.—Room Z.

Model lotus bud, with ornamentation similar to No. 46456.

QUALITY OF GLAZE, poor; colour, medium blue.

Tip of bud broken off.

46460. **Model Lotus Bud** [6].—Blue glazed faïence.—Height 0 m ·085.—Maximum diameter 0 m ·032.—Room D.

Model lotus bud, with ornamentation similar to No. 46456.

A hole has been sunk in the centre of the broad end, in which are remains of a wooden pin.

QUALITY OF GLAZE, medium ; colour, medium blue.

46461. **Model Lotus Bud** [7].—Blue glazed faïence.—Height 0 m ·095.—Maximum diameter 0 m ·035.—Room D.

Model lotus bud, with sepals outlined in black and hairs represented by short black lines: a row of shorter sepals around the base.

QUALITY OF GLAZE, good ; colour, light blue.

46462. **Tip of a model Lotus Bud** [8].—Blue glazed faïence.—Room D.

Tip of a model lotus bud, with ornamentation similar to that of No. 46456.

QUALITY OF GLAZE, good ; colour, medium blue.

46463. **Lower end of a model Lotus Bud** [9].—Blue glazed faïence.—Maximum diameter 0 m ·032.—Room D.

Lower end of a model lotus bud, with ornamentation similar to that of No. 46456.

QUALITY OF GLAZE, blue ; colour, medium blue.

24. MODEL KOHL POTS.

—   **Model Kohl Pot** [1].—Blue glazed faïence.—Height 0 m ·075.—
Diameter at base 0 m ·02.—Room D.—Plate XXVI [1].

Model kohl pot, in the shape of a hollow shaft with capital composed of finely
modelled palm leaves tied round with three rings of cord. On the column two
vertical lines of hieroglyphs, written in black, reading :

QUALITY OF GLAZE, very fine ; colour, a brilliant dark blue.

[Davis Collection.]

46464. **Model Kohl Pot** [2].—Blue glazed faïence.—Height 0 m ·07.—
Diameter at the base 0 m ·015.—Room D.

Model kohl pot, in shape and ornamentation similar to No. [1], but without the
modelled bands round the upper part of the shaft, black painted bands being in
their place. No inscription.

QUALITY OF GLAZE, good ; colour, a dark blue.

46465. **Model Kohl Pot** [3].—Blue glazed faïence.—Height 0 m ·065.—
Diameter at base 0 m ·015.—Room D.

Model kohl pot, in shape and ornamentation similar to No. 46464.

QUALITY OF GLAZE, good ; colour, a dark blue.

46466. **Lower part of a model Kohl Pot** [4].—Blue glazed faïence.—
Diameter at the base 0 m ·02.

Model kohl pot, in shape similar to shaft of No. 1. Inscription on side written
vertically in black :

QUALITY OF GLAZE, very fine ; colour, a brilliant dark blue.

46467. Two fragments of a model Kohl Pot [5].—Blue glazed faïence.—
Height 0 m ·09.—Diameter at base 0 m ·025.—Room R.

Model kohl pot, in the shape of a hollow shaft with capital composed of finely
modelled palm leaves, having a square abacus at the top.

QUALITY OF GLAZE, fine ; colour, dark blue.

46468. Four fragments of a model Kohl Pot [6].—Blue glazed faïence.—
Diameter at base 0 m ·017.

Fragments of a model kohl pot, similar to No. 46467, but without the square abacus.

QUALITY OF GLAZE, good ; colour, dark blue.

25. MODEL HEADS OF SERPENTS.

46469. Model Head of a Serpent [1].—Blue glazed faïence.—Length 0 m ·05.—Maximum width across head, 0 m ·023.—Room D.

Head of a serpent, finely modelled, with the prenomen of Thoutmôsis IV on the top of head : (⊙ 𓎗 |).

QUALITY OF GLAZE, fine; colour, dark blue.

46470. Model Head of a Serpent [2].—Blue glazed faïence.—Maximum width across head 0 m ·022.—Room D.

Model head of a serpent, in shape and inscription similar to No. 46469.

QUALITY OF GLAZE, good; colour, dark blue.

Broken off at end.

46471. Model Head of a Serpent [3].—Blue glazed faïence.—Length 0 m ·035.—Maximum diameter 0 m ·012.—Room D.

Head of a serpent, finely modelled in blue glazed faïence, with black dots and lines round neck, and black eyes.

QUALITY OF GLAZE, good; colour, dark blue.

Pierced at end for suspension.

46472. Model Head of a Serpent [4].—Blue glazed faïence.—Length 0 m ·035.—Maximum diameter 0 m ·012.—Room D.

Model head of a serpent, in shape and ornamentation similar to No. 46471.

QUALITY OF GLAZE, good; colour, dark blue.

Pierced at end for suspension.

46473. Model Head of a Serpent [5].—Blue glazed faïence.—Length 0 m ·035.—Maximum diameter 0 m ·012.—Room D.

Model head of a serpent, in shape and ornamentation similar to No. 46471.

QUALITY OF GLAZE, good; colour, dark blue.

Pierced at end for suspension.

46474. **Model Head of a Serpent** [6].—Blue glazed faïence.—Length 0 m ·035.—Maximum diameter 0 m ·012.—Room D.

Head of a serpent, finely modelled in blue glazed faïence, with black dots and lines round neck and eyes.

QUALITY OF GLAZE, very good; colour, dark blue.

Broken into two pieces.

26. MISCELLANEOUS AMULETS.

46475. Amulet [1].—Blue glazed faïence.—Length 0 m ·115.—Width 0 m ·04.—Thickness 0 m ·013.—Room D.—Plate XXVI.

〈〉-shaped amulet, in blue glazed faïence, flat at the back and slightly rounded on its upper surface. It bears the prenomen of Thoutmôsis IV within a cartouche without base line in the centre of the upper side.

QUALITY OF GLAZE, medium; colour, medium blue.

Perfect.

— **Amulet** [2].—Blue glazed faïence.—Length 0 m ·115.—Width 0 m ·045.—Thickness 0 m ·01.—Room D.

〈〉-shaped amulet, in blue glazed faïence. Plain.

QUALITY OF GLAZE, medium; colour, medium blue.

Broken into two pieces (complete).

[Davis Collection.]

46476. Amulet [3].—Blue glazed faïence.—Length 0 m ·12.—Width 0 m ·045.—Thickness 0 m ·01.—Room D.

〈〉-shaped amulet, similar to No. [2].

QUALITY OF GLAZE, medium; colour, medium blue.

Broken into two pieces (complete).

46477. Amulet [4].—Blue glazed faïence.—Length 0 m ·11.—Width 0 m ·04.—Thickness 0 m ·01.—Room D.

〈〉-shaped amulet, similar to No. [2].

QUALITY OF GLAZE, medium; colour, medium blue.

Broken into two pieces (complete).

46478. Amulet [5].—Blue glazed faïence.—Length 0 m ·11.—Width 0 m ·037.—Thickness 0 m ·01.—Room **D.**

◊-shaped amulet, similar to No. [2].

QUALITY OF GLAZE, medium ; colour, medium blue.

Broken into three pieces.

46479. Amulet [6].—Blue glazed faïence.—Length 0 m ·11.—Width 0 m ·04.—Thickness 0 m ·01.—Room **D.**

◊-shaped amulet, similar to No. [2].

QUALITY OF GLAZE, medium ; colour, medium blue.

Broken into two pieces.

— **Amulet** [7].—Blue glazed faïence.—Length 0 m ·11.—Width 0 m ·04.—Thickness 0 m ·01.—Room **D.**

◊-shaped amulet, similar to No. [2].

QUALITY OF GLAZE, medium ; colour, medium blue.

Broken into two pieces.

[Davis Collection.]

46480. Amulet [8].—Blue glazed faïence.—Length 0 m ·11.—Width 0 m ·043.—Thickness 0 m ·01.—Room **D.**

◊-shaped amulet, similar to No. [2].

QUALITY OF GLAZE, medium ; colour, medium blue.

Broken into two pieces.

46481. Fragment of an Amulet [9].—Blue glazed faïence.—Width 0 m ·04.—Thickness 0 m ·01.

Fragment of a ◊-shaped amulet, similar to No. [2].

QUALITY OF GLAZE, medium ; colour, medium blue.

46482. Fragment of an Amulet [10].—Blue glazed faïence.—Width 0 m ·04.—Thickness 0 m ·01.

Fragment of a ◊-shaped amulet, similar to No. [2].

QUALITY OF GLAZE, medium ; colour, medium blue.

46483. **Amulet** [11].—Blue glazed faïence.—Height 0 m ·065.—Width 0 m ·025.—Thickness 0 m ·0025.—Room D.

◯-shaped amulet, in blue glazed faïence, flat at the back and rounded on its upper surface.

QUALITY OF GLAZE, good; colour, medium blue.

Broken at the top.

46484. **Fragment of an Amulet** [12].—Blue glazed faïence.—Width 0 m ·08. —Thickness 0 m ·0025.—Room D.

Fragment of the centre part of an amulet, similar to No. 46483.

QUALITY OF GLAZE, good; colour, medium blue.

46485. **Fragment of an Amulet** [13].—Blue glazed faïence.—Width 0 m ·011.—Thickness 0 m ·004.—Room D.

Fragment of the upper part of an amulet, similar to No. 46483.

—   **Amulet** [14].—Blue glazed faïence.—Height 0 m ·065.—Breadth across arms 0 m ·03.—Room D.—Plate XXVI [14].

Amulet, in the form of the symbol of life ☥, rounded on its upper surface, flat below and with a cylindrical bead at the top for suspension. The centre of the loop is solid and painted black.

QUALITY OF GLAZE, very fine; colour, a brilliant deep blue.

Broken into two pieces (complete).

[Davis Collection.]

—   **Fragments of Amulets** [15].—Blue glazed faïence.—Room D.

Sixty fragments of amulets, similar to No. [14], except that some of them have the centre of the loop hollow.

[Davis Collection.]

—   **Amulet** [16].—Blue glazed faïence.—Height 0 m ·05.—Breadth across arms 0 m ·025.—Room D.—Plate XXVI [16].

Amulet, in the form of the symbol of protection ♎, rounded and modelled on its upper surface, flat below. The centre of the loop is hollow.

QUALITY OF GLAZE, very fine; colour, a brilliant deep blue.

Broken into two pieces (complete).

[Davis Collection.]

— **Fragments of Amulets** [17].—Blue glazed faïence.—Room D.

Seventy-two fragments of amulets, similar to No. [16], except that some of them have the centre of the loop solid and painted black.

[Davis Collection.]

— **Amulet** [18].—Blue glazed faïence.—Height 0 m ·05.—Breadth 0 m ·02.—Room D.—Plate XXVI [18].

Amulet, in the form of the symbol of stability ☩, modelled in low relief above, flat below. At the top is fixed a cylindrical bead for attachment.

QUALITY OF GLAZE, very fine; colour, a brilliant deep blue.

Perfect.

[Davis Collection.]

— **Fragments of Amulets** [19].—Blue glazed faïence.—Room D.

Seventy fragments of amulets, similar to No. [18], but varying slightly in size.

[Davis Collection.]

— **Fragments of Amulets** [20].—Blue glazed faïence.—Room D.

Eleven fragments of amulets, in the form of the sacred eye 𓂀, modelled above in low relief, flat below. These amulets were originally about 0 m ·04 in length.

[Davis Collection.]

— **Beads** [21].—Blue glazed faïence and glass.—Room D and Chamber 3.

A small quantity of blue and violet faïence beads and blue glass beads were also found.

[Davis Collection.]

46486. Group of Amulets in Stand [22].— Blue glazed faïence.—Room D.— Plate XXVI.

Group of three amulets, 𓊽, 𓋹, 𓊽, in a stand. Each amulet is modelled in low relief in front and is flat at the back. They are all ornamented with black lines. At the base of each amulet is a tongue to fix it into the mortice holes of the stand.

The 𓊽-amulet is broken across the top and a fragment from it is wanting. In breadth it measures 0 m ·038.

The 𓋹-amulet is 0 m ·115 high and it has its left arm broken away.

The 𓊽-amulet is broken above the first bar and the whole of the top is missing.

The base is rounded at the ends but is flat in section, and measures 0 m ·1 long, 0 m ·022 broad, by 0 m ·008 thick.

QUALITY OF GLAZE, medium; colour, medium blue.

— **Group of Amulets in Stand** [23].—Blue glazed faïence.—Room D.

Group of three amulets, ⚊, ⚊, ⚊, in a stand. Each amulet is modelled in low relief in front and is flat at the back; they were all ornamented with black lines. At the base of each amulet is a tongue to fix it into the mortice holes of the stand.

The ⚊-amulet is broken across the bottom. In height it measures 0 m ·085, and its maximum breadth is 0 m ·035.

Of the ⚊-amulet only the top is preserved.

The ⚊-amulet is broken across the top and measures in breadth 0 m ·032.

The base is rectangular in shape, is flat in section and measures 0 m ·135 long, 0 m ·04 broad, by 0 m ·0012.

QUALITY OF GLAZE, good; colour, medium blue.

Bears traces of ancient mending.

[Davis Collection.]

46487. Group of Amulets in Stand [24].—Blue glazed faïence.—Room D.

Group of three amulets, ⚊, ⚊, ⚊, in a stand. Each amulet is modelled in low relief and is flat at the back; they were all ornamented with black lines. At the base of each amulet is a tongue to fix it into the mortice holes of the stand.

The left-hand ⚊-amulet is broken across the top, and in breadth is 0 m ·035.

The centre ⚊-amulet is broken across the top and in breadth measures 0 m ·035.

The ⚊-amulet measures 0 m ·08 high and its maximum breadth is 0 m ·04.

The base is rectangular in shape, is flat in section, and measures 0 m ·13 long, 0 m ·04 broad, and 0 m ·0015 thick.

QUALITY OF GLAZE, good; colour, a medium blue.

Bears traces of having been anciently mended with yellow plaster.

PLATE XXVII.

[1]   46488.

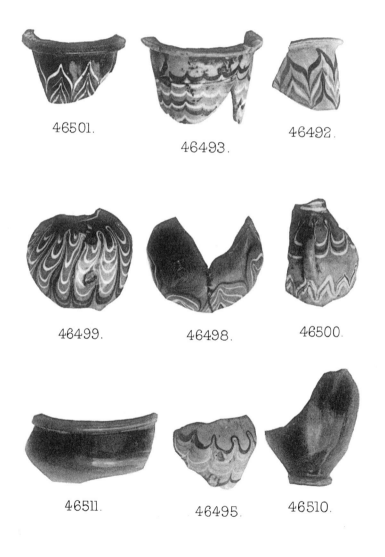

46501.   46492.

46493.

46499.   46498.   46500.

46511.   46495.   46510.

GLASS.

27. GLASS.

— **Bottle** [1].—Light turquoise-blue glass.—Height 0 m ·09.—Maximum diameter of bowl 0 m ·06.—Room D.—Plate XXVII [1].

In the shape of a broad-bowled bottle, with narrow neck and projecting rim, and foot and projecting base.

ORNAMENTATION: *Rim of lip*, violet; *neck*, zigzag lines of yellow, violet, light blue violet, white, violet, light blue, white, light blue, and yellow; *bowl*, light blue ground with zigzag lines of yellow, light blue, and white three times repeated and a violet zigzag line below (the two glass loop handles broken away); *foot* and *base*, light blue.

QUALITY OF GLASS, very fine.

Eleven pieces (incomplete).

[Davis Collection.]

46488. **Bottle** [2].—Light turquoise-blue glass.—Height 0 m ·07 ?—Maximum diameter of bowl 0 m ·05.—Room D.—Plate XXVII.

In the shape of a broad-bowled bottle with wide neck and projecting base.

ORNAMENTATION: *Rim of lip*, yellow; *neck*, wavy lines of dark blue, light blue and yellow; *bowl*, light blue with dark blue loop handles (broken) on sides; *base*, light blue.

QUALITY OF GLASS, very good.

Nine pieces (incomplete).

46489. **Fragments of the lower part of a Vase** [3].—Light turquoise-blue glass.—Diameter of foot 0 m ·03.—Room D.

In the shape of a long slender vase with foot and projecting base; the lip and neck are wanting.

ORNAMENTATION: *bowl*, light blue with zigzag lines of white, violet, and yellow lines; around the lower extremity of the bowl is a rim of violet; *foot* and *base*, light blue.

QUALITY OF GLASS, very fine.

Eight pieces (incomplete).

46490.   Fragments of a Vase [4].—Light turquoise-blue glass.—Diameter of foot 0 m ·03.—Room D.

In the form of a broad-necked vase.

ORNAMENTATION: *Lip*, light blue; *neck*, zigzag lines of white, dark blue, light blue and yellow repeated four times with a yellow zigzag line below; *bowl*, light blue, with (broken) violet loop handles; *foot*, light blue with a rim of yellow.

QUALITY OF GLASS, very good.

Nine pieces.

46491.   Fragments of a Vase [5].—Light turquoise-blue glass.—Maximum diameter of bowl 0 m ·055.—Room D.

In the form of a broad-necked vase.

ORNAMENTATION: *Lip*, violet rim; *neck*, alternate bands of yellow, light blue, violet, light blue, and white zigzag lines; *bowl*, light blue with wavy bands at top turning to zigzag bands below, of repeating yellow, dark blue, light blue, and white lines; *foot*, light blue with violet rim around base.

QUALITY OF GLASS, very good.

Five pieces.

46492.   Fragments of a Vase [6].—Light turquoise-blue glass.—Room D.— Plate XXVII.

In the form of a broad-necked vase.

ORNAMENTATION: *Lip*, violet rim; *neck*, zigzag bands of violet, yellow, violet, light blue, violet, light blue, and white lines twice repeated; *bowl*, light blue with zigzag bands of yellow, light blue, white, light blue, yellow, light blue and white lines.

QUALITY OF GLASS, very good.

Six pieces.

46493.   Fragments of a Vase [7].—Light turquoise-blue glass.—Diameter across neck 0 m ·06.—Room D.—Plate XXVII.

In the form of a broad-necked vase with rim round neck.

ORNAMENTATION: *Lip*, violet rim; *neck*, wavy bands of yellow, violet, light blue, and white lines, twice repeated; *bowl*, light turquoise-blue glass with a similar arrangement of coloured bands as on neck.

QUALITY OF GLASS, very good.

Twelve pieces.

46494. Fragments of a Vase [8].—Light turquoise-blue glass.—Diameter of foot 0 m ·035.—Room D.

In the form of a broad-necked vase with rim round neck.

ORNAMENTATION: *Lip*, violet rim; *neck*, ⋎⋎⋎ bands of white, dark blue, light blue, and dark blue lines; *bowl*, light turquoise-blue glass with violet, light blue, white, light blue, violet ⋎⋎⋎ lines twice repeated; *handles*, dark blue; *foot*, light blue.

QUALITY OF GLASS, very good.

Four pieces.

46495. Fragments of a Vase [9].—Light turquoise-blue glass.—Room D.— Plate XXVII.

Fragment of the bowl of a broad-necked vase.

ORNAMENTATION: *Bowl*, wavy lines of yellow, light blue, violet, white, light blue, violet, white, light blue, violet, and yellow on a light blue ground; *handles*, dark blue glass.

QUALITY OF GLASS, very good.

One piece.

46496. Fragments of a Vase [10].—Light turquoise-blue glass.—Room D.

Fragments of the lower part of a small vase, in light blue glass with thick rim round neck. Plain.

QUALITY OF GLASS, very good.

Eight pieces.

46497. Fragments of a Vase [11].—Light turquoise-blue glass.—Diameter across neck 0 m ·06.—Room D.

Fragments of a small vase, in light blue glass with a rim of yellow glass around the top of the neck.

QUALITY OF GLASS, very good.

Five pieces.

46498. Fragments of a Vase [12].—Violet glass.—Maximum diameter of bowl 0 m ·06.—Chamber 4.—Plate XXVII.

Fragments of the bowl of a broad-necked vase.

ORNAMENTATION: *Bowl*, wavy lines of yellow, violet, white, and violet repeated four times on a violet ground.

QUALITY OF GLASS, very good.

Two pieces.

Catal. du Musée, n. 46001.

46499. Fragment of a Vase [13].—Violet glass.—Maximum diameter of bowl about 0 m ·06.—Room D.—Plate XXVII.

Fragments of the bowl of a broad-necked vase.

ORNAMENTATION : *Bowl*, a wavy line of yellow, then five white wavy lines alternating with violet lines; below, are two yellow wavy lines alternating with violet; *handle*, violet glass.

QUALITY OF GLASS, good.

One piece.

46500. Fragments of a Bottle [14].—Violet glass.—Diameter across neck 0 m ·03.—Room D.—Plate XXVII.

Fragments of bottle.

ORNAMENTATION : *Lip*, yellow rim; *neck*, rings of white alternating with violet; *bowl*, wavy lines of white, violet, yellow, violet, and white on a dark blue ground; *handle*, violet.

QUALITY OF GLASS, very good.

Three pieces.

46501. Fragments of a Vase [15].—Violet glass.—Diameter across neck 0 m ·055.—Room D.—Plate XXVII.

Fragments of a broad-necked vase.

ORNAMENTATION : *Lip* and *rim*, violet; *neck*, ⋙ lines of white, violet, yellow, white, violet, yellow, white, violet, repeated twice; *bowl*, similar ornamentation as on neck.

QUALITY OF GLASS, very good.

Four pieces.

46502. Fragments of a Bowl [16].—Violet glass.—Room D.

Fragments of a circular-shaped bowl, with small foot.

ORNAMENTATION : *Lip*, rim of yellow; *bowl*, wavy lines of yellow, violet, white, violet, repeated four times and on the base a line of yellow.

QUALITY OF GLASS, very good.

Five pieces.

46503. Fragments of a Vase [17].—Violet glass.—Room D.

Fragments of a broad-necked vase.

ORNAMENTATION : *Rim of neck*, violet; *neck*, wavy lines of yellow, violet, white, violet. yellow, repeated twice.

QUALITY OF GLASS, very good.

Two pieces.

46504. Fragments of a Vase [18].—Violet glass.—Room D.

Fragments of a vase.

ORNAMENTATION: *Bowl*, shallow wavy lines of white, blue, and yellow, on a violet ground.

QUALITY OF GLASS, good.

Three small pieces.

46505. Fragment of a Vase [19].—Violet glass.—Room D.

Fragment of a bowl of a vase.

ORNAMENTATION: *Bowl*, wavy lines of light blue, violet, white, violet, and yellow, twice repeated on a blue ground.

QUALITY OF GLASS, very good.

One small piece.

46506. Fragment of a Vase [20].—Transparent dark blue glass.—Room D.

Fragment of the bowl of a vase.

ORNAMENTATION: *Bowl*, wavy ⋁⋁ lines of white, blue, yellow, white, twice repeated on a dark blue ground.

QUALITY OF GLASS, very good.

One small piece.

46507. Fragments of a Bottle [21].—Violet glass.—Diameter across neck 0 m ·027.—Room D.

Fragments of a glass bottle, with narrow foot.

ORNAMENTATION: *Rim of neck*, plain; *neck*, one white band around it; *bowl*, plain; *foot*, a white rim round it.

QUALITY OF GLASS, very good.

Three pieces.

46508. Fragments of a Bottle [22].—Violet glass.—Diameter across mouth 0 m ·03.—Room D.

Fragments of a bottle, with broad bowl and narrow foot.

ORNAMENTATION: *Rim of neck*, yellow; *neck*, plain; *bowl*, plain; *foot*, plain with a yellow rim around.

QUALITY OF GLASS, very good.

Two pieces.

46509. Fragments of a Vase [23].—Violet glass.—Diameter across neck 0 m ·055.—Room D.

Fragments of a broad-necked vase.

ORNAMENTATION: *Rim of neck*, light blue; *neck*, plain; *bowl*, plain; *handle,* yellow.

QUALITY OF GLASS, good.

Two pieces.

46510. Fragments of a Vase [24].—Violet glass.—Room D.—Plate XXVII.

Fragments of the lower part of a bottle, with flat bottom.   Plain violet glass.

QUALITY OF GLASS, very good.

Two pieces.

46511. Fragments of a Bowl [25].—Violet glass.—Diameter across mouth 0 m ·09.—Room D.—Plate XXVII.

Fragments of a shallow bowl, with narrow rim, plain violet glass.

QUALITY OF GLASS, good.

Six pieces.

46512. Fragments of a Bowl [26.]—Violet glass.—Room D.

Fragments of a bowl, similar to No. 46511.

Two pieces.

46513. Fragments of a Vase [27].—Violet glass.—Room D.

Fragments of a large glass vase, with yellow rim on lip.

QUALITY OF GLASS, good.

Five pieces.

46514. Fragments of a Vase [28].—Violet glass.—Room D.

Fragments of a large broad-necked vase.

ORNAMENTATION: *Neck*, rim of yellow glass; *neck* and *bowl*, plain.

QUALITY OF GLASS, good.

Eleven pieces.

46515. Fragments of a Vase [29].—Violet glass.—Room D.

Fragments of a large broad-necked vase.

ORNAMENTATION: The bowl is plain, with handles on either side composed of thick yellow rods.

QUALITY OF GLASS, good.

Three pieces.

46516. Fragments of a Vase [30].—Milky coloured glass.—Room D.

Fragments of a vase, of milky coloured glass without ornamentation.

QUALITY OF GLASS, fair.

Six pieces.

46517. Foot of a Bowl [31].—Brown glass.—Diameter 0 m ·042.—Room D.

Fragment of a large bowl, with narrow foot, in brown coloured glass.

QUALITY OF GLASS, medium.

Ten pieces.

46518. Foot of a Bowl [32].—Brown glass.—Diameter 0 m ·055.—Room D.

Foot of a large bowl, similar to No. 46517.

One piece.

46519. Fragments of a Dish [33].—Brown glass.—Room D.

Fragments of a brown glass shallow dish, ground on both sides.

Twenty-three pieces.

46520. Fragments of a Bracelet [34].—Violet glass.—Diameter 0 m ·07.— Width 0 m ·02.—Room D.

Fragments of bracelet, of violet glass, with rims of white opaque glass.

QUALITY OF GLASS, medium.

Four pieces.

46521. Fragments of Bracelet [35].—Violet glass.—Diameter 0 m ·08.— Width 0 m ·025.—Room D.

Fragments of a violet glass bracelet, with two rims of yellow glass.

QUALITY OF GLASS, good.

Two pieces.

46522.   Fragment of a Bracelet [36].—Violet glass.—Width 0 m ·02.— Room D.

Fragment of a similar bracelet to No. 46521.

46523.   Fragments of a Bowl [37].—Light blue glass.—Room D.

Fragments of a bowl, of light blue glass, with a rim of lighter blue.
QUALITY OF GLASS, good.
Two pieces.

46524.   Fragments of a Bowl [38].—Light blue glass.—Room D.

Fragments of a bowl, light blue glass, with yellow rim.
QUALITY OF GLASS, good.
Six pieces.

46525.   Eighty-five miscellaneous Fragments [39].—Of coloured glass.

PLATE XXVIII.

TAPESTRY-WOVEN FRAGMENTS.

TAPESTRY-WOVEN FABRICS.

THESE fragments[1] are of supreme importance in the history of tapestry-weaving. Bearing the cartouche of Amenôthes II, they are about 1000 years earlier in date than the oldest tapestry-woven fabrics hitherto known, viz., the fragments dating from about 400 B.C., found in the Crimea, and now preserved in the Hermitage at St. Petersburg. This superb workmanship proves that tapestry-weaving was in a high state of perfection in the reign of Amenôthes II, and the technique is most interesting. The texture is very fine for tapestry, the warp-strings numbering about sixty in the space of one inch. In the larger piece, these run vertically as one reads the hieroglyphs; in the smaller pieces, horizontally; in all three, they are looser in some parts than in others, to which the warp owes its undulative appearance. The weft is appreciably thicker than the warp, and the delicacy with which floral and other forms are rendered leaves no doubt that an upright loom was used. This is confirmed by the fact that the patterns are exactly the same on both sides, there being no "passings" or ends of threads visible, and probably the weaver sat in front of the loom instead of behind it. The warp bears evidence of having been relaxed or tightened at will, in places where its direction would aid the execution of the pattern—as in weaving the vultures, where the warps are curved to enable the wing, etc., to be more easily rendered. A loom in which the warp-strings are kept taut by a series of weights, instead of being fastened to a cylinder, would admit of this technique, and this was the principle of the Scandinavian and Greek looms. One of the latter is represented on a vase designed about 400 B.C. and found at Chiusi. In the smallest fragment, the forearm of the hieroglyph ⌣⌐ resembles needlework in its execution, but most likely it has been woven by a method common in Coptic work. Another characteristic of Coptic tapestry is that the weft, instead of being at right angles to the warp, often crosses it obliquely to describe a curve. This is the method employed in executing the hieroglyph ⌇, the weaving being begun at the middle of the base and the form built up by a series of concentric layers of weft threads. Except for these instances, there is but little difference between the technique of these ancient fragments and the methods of our day. We can see, in the spaces between contiguous warps bearing different colours, the crossing stitch at intervals which, then as now, was necessary to prevent the fabric coming apart. The colours are red, blue, green, yellow, brown or black, and a grey. Of these, the reds and blues are very bright; the brown or black has perished, leaving the bare warp-strings, but, here and there, particles of it remain.—[W. G. THOMSON.]

46526. **Portion of a Robe of Amenôthes II** [1].—Linen.—Height 0 m ·29.—Length 0 m ·42.—Chamber 3.—Plate I [Frontispiece].

Portion of a white linen robe, with ornaments tapestry-woven in coloured linen threads. The designs consist of (1) eight rows of ⚕ lotus flowers in blue and red,

---

[1] For the following remarks we are indebted to Mr. W. G. Thomson, who studied the fragments with a view to writing a report on them.

alternating with ☥ papyrus infloresences in blue, red, yellow and brown outlined in black. To the left of these rows of flowers is (2) the prenomen [⊙🜊🜕] of Amenôthes II within a cartouche; on either side are crowned uræi delicately worked in blue, brown, black, red, and yellow coloured threads. On the left-hand side the uræus wears the red crown of Lower Egypt, on the right the white crown (outlined red) of Upper Egypt. Above the cartouche are given the titles of the king : 🜚. Below the cartouche is a large ⌇-sign beautifully worked in red, blue, green, and yellow coloured threads.

On the left-hand edge of this portion of the robe is a very delicately wrought border (0 m ·018 in width) of alternate lotus flowers and buds, divided from the rest of the garment by a row of fine black stitches of needlework. These flowers are tapestry-woven in red, blue, and green linen threads, the buds in red, brown, and black linen threads.

On the right-hand edge is a border (0 m ·018 in width) consisting of a double row of alternating truncated discs, tapestry-woven in red and blue linen threads, divided from the rest of the garment by black stitches of needlework. This edge of the robe has been strengthened by being " bound " with coarsish stitches in white linen thread.

46527. **Fragment of a Garment** [2].—Linen.—Height 0 m ·20.—Width 0 m ·085.—Chamber 3.—Plate XXVIII.

Fragment of a white linen garment, with a hieroglyphic inscription tapestry-woven in various coloured linen threads. The inscription, written vertically, reads :

.

46528. **Fragment of a Garment** [3].—Linen.—Height 0 m ·12.—Width 0 m ·035.—Chamber 3.—Plate XXVIII.

Fragment of a white linen garment, with the *ka*-name of Thoutmôsis III tapestry-woven in various coloured linen threads. The inscription, written vertically, reads :

46529. **Portion of a Garment** [4].—Linen.—Height 0 m ·46.—Length 0 m ·25.—Chamber 3.—Plate XXVIII.

Portion of a garment, coarsely woven in linen threads (warp 25 threads, woof 30 threads to 1 mm.), and divided vertically into fourteen narrow bands (each about 0 m ·018 wide) by thick double threads of linen dyed pink and woven into the material. The four bands on the right-hand side are plain, the remaining ten are ornamented with rosettes wrought in needlework, each rosette being composed of a pale green centre with six pale pink petals, except in the thirteenth row, where pink rosettes alternate with green petaled rosettes with pink centres.

PRESERVATION : much decayed.

LIST OF PLATES.

LIST OF ILLUSTRATIONS IN THE TEXT.

INDEX.

HARRISON AND SONS, PRINTERS IN ORDINARY TO HIS MAJESTY, LONDON, W.C.

ALSO AVAILABLE IN THE SERIES...

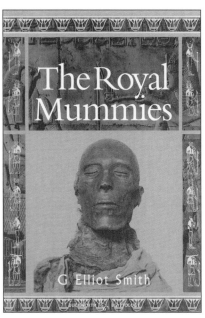

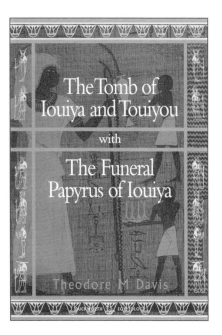

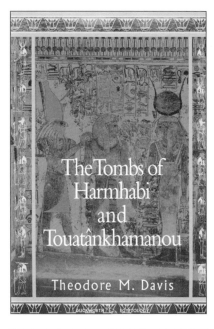

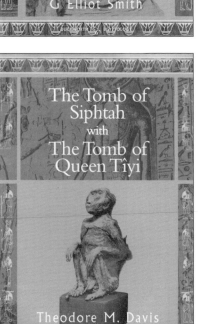

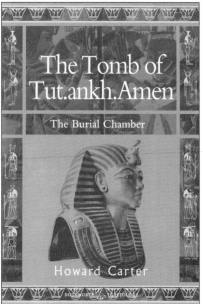

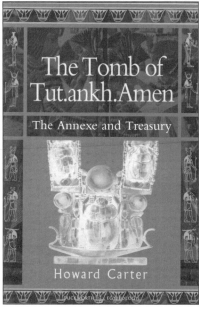